Like Father

*The biographies of
the Rt Hon*

Lord Justice Robert Lush, PC

*and his son,
the Rt Hon*

Sir Charles Montague Lush, PC

Baron Charlie Lush

First published in Great Britain by Charlie Lush Books, 1999
This revised edition published in Great Britain by
Charlie Lush Books, 2015

© Charlie Lush Books, 2015

All rights reserved. No part of this publication may be reproduced, stored in a retrieval system, or transmitted, in any form or by any means, electronic, mechanical, photocopying, recording or otherwise, without the prior permission of Baron Lush.

Acknowledgements

My special thanks to Robert and Violet Nuttall (née Lush), Dr Robin and Brenda Lush, Sir Godfray and Susan Le Quesne, Frances Holman (née Locock), Dr Gordon Lush, Fred Thomson, Sir Adrian Swire, Theresa Thom, the Admiral Blake Museum, the Headmasters of Orley Farm School and Westminster School, and the Somerset, Wiltshire, Dorset and Berkshire Record Offices without whose assistance this publication would not have been possible.

In loving memory of

*Violet and Robert Nuttall
and
Susan and Godfray Le Quesne*

Contents

The Rt Hon Lord Justice and Lady Lush

Chapter One, *Tilling the Soil* — page 7

Chapter Two, *Sowing Seeds* — 23

Chapter Three, *Harvesting the Crop* — 47

The Rt Hon Sir Charles Montague Lush

Chapter Four, *New Beginnings* — 67

Chapter Five, *A Unique Figure at the Bar* — 89

Chapter Six, *The Little Man with a Big Reputation* — 117

Postlude — 141

Appendix — 142

Virtute non astutia

The Rt Hon Lord Justice and Lady Lush

Chapter One

Tilling the Soil

> He gave his strength to the weak,
> His substance to the poor,
> His sympathy to the suffering
> And his heart to God

Charles Montague Lush

Firstly, my choice of title was taken from the *Vanity Fair* print of 1911 by Ape Junior, 'Like Father like Son.' When Robert Lush's son, Charles Montague, was raised to the Bench in 1910, it seemed likely that he would continue to follow in his father's footsteps. And in many respects, he did earning high acclaim from his friends and colleagues for his legal acumen and Christian philanthropy and becoming a Privy Councillor himself in 1925. But as we shall discover in the course of this book, 'Montie' was no carbon copy of his father nor could he be expected to be after all the radical reforms of his father's age and the impact of the First World War. Nonetheless, there can be little doubt that Robert would have been just as proud of his son's achievements as his own father was of his and both stories have been equally fascinating to research.

However, before I explore their lives in greater detail, I would be failing in my duty as a family historian if I neglected to mention some of the family's earlier roots to establish from where Robert had emerged. The first recorded spelling of the family name is shown to be that of a William Lussier at the *Assize Court* of Somerset in 1243 and it would appear that the name is derived from the French words *le huissier*, meaning 'the usher' or 'doorkeeper'. Interestingly, an area of the Wiltshire/Dorset border that includes Donhead, Tisbury and Teffont Magna has been a prime location for the Lushes certainly since the early 14th century and there are written records claiming that the Donhead community crossed the Channel with William the Conqueror. Once he had established his new kingdom in England, William's army was disbanded at Old Sarum, not many miles away from Donhead, so it is quite possible that some of his soldiers would have settled there and that some of them might easily have been Lushes or, perhaps more accurately, Lussiers.

Another early record in the VCH for Wiltshire refers to Messrs John, Richard and Robert Lush as farmers of Totterdale circa 1330 which would tally with the first entry on Robert's original family tree: 'Robert Lusshe of Compton St Martins, Somerset, Gentleman tempus Henry VIII and seventh in descent from John le Lufshe of Tyfesbury, Wiltshire, who paid the subsidy on his lands there in 1330.' Also from the same area, there are early records relating to an Edward Lusch of Melberye Abbas and a Dr Lushe of Aiesbury. The former was involved in a conspiracy to rob Richard Applin at Christmas time, 1532, but it appears that his part was solely confined to selling a mare to the robbers. And seven years later, the latter, who was Vicar of Aiesbury at the time, was reported to the Lord Privy Seal, Thomas Cromwell, for apparent papist sympathies and possessing 'books of impotinacy.' One of these books was called *Egisippus and Clifus* and appears to have been a collection of sermons, including one by Thomas Becket. Nevertheless, the man who confiscated them obviously had to give them a good read before handing them over to the authorities because he wrote in his report, 'Have not time to look into the others, they are so evil written, but have taken them home to read.' They must have been very entertaining!

From Donhead, there basically emerged three lines of Lushes settling on the Wiltshire/Dorset border, in Somerset and at Sparsholt in Berkshire. (A brass with the inscription, 'Here lyeth buryed the bodie of Robert Loyshe of Sparsholt, Yeoman who deceased ye 26 of Ianuary, 1605' was only recently discovered in *Holy Rood Church*, Sparsholt, in 1992 and there are three other Lush memorials in the aisle.) These lines then subdivided – Arthur and William Lush of Bridport were exiled to Barbados in 1685, following the unsuccessful Monmouth Rebellion – and it is perhaps worth mentioning here that Robert was not the only Lush from rural England to make his way up to London during the early part of the nineteenth century. However, despite the fact that a combination of early reforms, the plight of the agricultural labourers in the 1830's and the growth of London's commercial base must have provided a certain impetus to emigrate to the City, even on foot, very few of his 'cousins' managed to achieve anything like the same sort of success. Certainly John Alfred Lush, MD, Liberal MP and Mayor of Salisbury earned more than just a penny or two out of his joint ownership of four lunatic asylums in London as well as another two in the Salisbury area with Corbin Finch and is known to have entertained the Prince of Wales at a banquet in September, 1872. (One of these asylums, just outside Salisbury still exists as a mental institution and John's elder son, Alfred, was admitted to *Gray's Inn* only three months after Montie.) In Kent, a third cousin of Robert's, James Robert Lush (1828-1898) became Mayor of Deal. And Silas William Lush, who had previously been paid 4d a day as a farm labourer in Dorset at the age of 18 in 1830, became the proprietor of coffee rooms in *Riding House Lane*, only a stone's throw from *All Souls*, Langham Place and not a great deal further from *Regent's Park Chapel* in Park Square East where, as we shall see, Robert and Elizabeth were destined to play a major role; it would be interesting to know whether or not they were aware of one another's presence. But there were others like another Robert and Daniel Lush who were not so fortunate and ended their days in the workhouse: the former died in 1863 at the workhouse in *York Street*, Westminster, and the latter in 1875 at the workhouse in *Mount St*, Grosvenor Square. Those of you who are at all familiar with the works of Charles Dickens will have some idea of what their lives must have been like.

So Robert's roots were on the farms of south Wiltshire but his destiny was evidently elsewhere. He was born at Tollard, near Shaftesbury, on the 25th October, 1807 to Robert Lush and Lucy Foote, daughter of Joseph Foote also of Tollard, but information about his childhood is scant and he seems to have been reluctant to elaborate. In a passage written after his death for the magazine *Life* by the novelist, Charles Reade, the description of Robert's early years is both sketchy and slightly misleading despite his obvious intention to praise our hero's achievements. For example, Reade states that when Robert's mother took him along to Chitty's office in Shaftesbury, she was a widow. This, in fact, was correct up to a point because she had previously been married to a William Wickham, who was buried at Donhead St Mary in 1802, but the statement implies that she was still a widow at this time which couldn't have been further from the truth. She had remarried Robert's father in 1806 and, by him, bore another ten children to add to her existing daughter, Susan. And secondly, he states that Robert was taken to the office at the age of twelve whereas his close friend, Dr Landels, indicates that his age was rather closer to sixteen. This might have simply been a novelist's ploy to disguise his lack of knowledge concerning Robert's early years or it might have been a kindly exaggeration but the fact still remains that we know precious little about Robert's upbringing or, indeed, the circumstances of his father. And to complicate matters even further, his father is described as a merchant on Robert's marriage certificate but as a gentleman on that of his brother William! However, having read through many accounts of Robert's life, I can testify that the gist of Reade's passage is sufficiently accurate in its description of how the young man secured his first job. The article is aptly entitled *Perseverance*:

'On a certain day in the year 1819, Mr Chitty, an attorney in Shaftesbury, was leaving his office for the day when he was met at the door by a respectable woman and a chubby-faced boy with a bright eye. He knew the woman slightly, a widow that kept a small stationer's shop in the town. She opened her business at once.

'Oh, Mr Chitty, I have brought you my Robert. He gives me no peace; his heart is set on being in a lawyer's office. But there, I have not got the money to apprentice him. Only we thought perhaps you could find some place or other for him, if it was ever so small.' Then she broke off and looked appealingly and the boy's cheeks and eyes were fired with expectation.

Most country towns at that time possessed two solicitors who might be called types: the old-established man, whose firm for generations had done the pacific and lucrative business – wills, settlements, partnerships, mortgages, etc. – and the sharp practitioner, who was the abler of the two at litigation and had to shake the plum tree instead of sitting under it and opening his mouth for the windfalls. Mr Chitty was No.2. But these sharp practitioners are often very good-natured and so, looking at the pleading widow and the beaming boy, he felt disposed to oblige them and rather sorry he could not. He said that his was a small office and he had no clerk's place vacant. 'And, indeed, if I had, he is too young. Why he is a mere child!'

'I am twelve next so-and-so,' said the boy, giving the month and the day.

'You don't look it, then,' said Mr Chitty incredulously.

'Indeed, but he is, sir,' said the widow. 'He never looked his age and writes a beautiful hand.'

'But I tell you I have no vacancy,' said Mr Chitty, turning dogged.

'Well, thank you, sir, all the same,' said the widow with the patience of her sex. 'Come, Robert, we mustn't detain the gentleman.'

So they turned away with disappointment marked on their faces, the boy's especially. Then Mr Chitty said, in a hesitating way, 'To be sure, there *is* a vacancy, but it is not the sort of thing for you.'

'What is it, sir, if you please?' asked the widow.

'Well, we want an office boy.'

'An office boy! What do you say, Robert? I suppose it is a beginning, sir. What will he have to do?'

'Why, sweep the office, run errands and carry papers, and that is not what he is after. Look at him! He has got that eye of his fixed on a counsellor's wig, you may depend, and sweeping a country attorney's office is not the stepping-stone to that.' He added warily, 'at least, there is no precedent reported.'

'La! sir,' said the widow, 'he only wants to turn an honest penny and be among law papers.'

'Aye, aye, to write 'em and sell 'em but not to dust 'em!'

'For that matter, sir, I believe he'd rather be the dust itself in your office than bide at home with me.' Here she turned angry with her offspring for half a moment.

'And so I would,' said the young master stoutly, endorsing his mother's hyperbole very boldly though his own mind was not of that kind which originates metaphors, similes, and engines of inaccuracy in general.'

'Then I say no more,' observed Mr Chitty; 'only mind, it is half-a-crown a week, that is all.'

The terms were accepted, and Master Robert entered on his humble duties. He was steady, persevering and pushing. In less than two years he got promoted to be a copying clerk. From this in due course he became a superior clerk. He studied, pushed and persevered till at last he became a fair practical lawyer and Mr Chitty's head clerk. And so much for Perseverance.

He remained some years in this position, trusted by his employer and respected too; for besides his special gifts as a law clerk, he was strict in morals and religious without parade.

In those days country attorneys could not fly to the metropolis and back to dinner. They relied much on London attorneys, their agents. Lawyer Chitty's agent was Mr Bishop, a judge's clerk, but in those days a judge's clerk had an insufficient stipend and was allowed to eke it out by private practice. Mr Bishop was agent to several country attorneys. Well, Chitty had a heavy case coming on at the assizes and asked Bishop to come down for once in a way and help him in person. Bishop did so and in working the case was delighted with Chitty's managing clerk. Before leaving he said that he sadly wanted a managing clerk he could rely on. Would Mr Chitty oblige him and part with this young man? Chitty made rather a wry face and said that young man was a pearl. 'I don't know what I shall do without him. Why, he is my *alter ego*.' However, he ended by saying generously that he would not stand in the young man's way. Then they had the clerk in and put the question to him. 'Sir,' said he, 'it is the ambition of my heart to go to London.'

Twenty-four hours after that our humble hero was installed in Mr Bishop's office, directing a large business in town and country. He filled that situation for many years, and got to be well-known in the legal profession. A brother of mine, who for years was one of a firm of solicitors in Lincoln's Inn Fields, remembers him well at this period and to have met him sometimes in his own chambers and sometimes in Judge's Chambers. My brother says he could not help noticing him for he bristled with intelligence, and knew a deal of law, though he looked a boy. The best of the joke is that this clerk afterwards turned out to be four years older than the solicitor who took him for a boy!

He was now amongst books as well as lawyers and studied closely the principles of law whilst the practice was sharpening him. He was much in the courts and every case there cited in argument or judgement he hunted out in the books and digested it, together with its application in practice by the living judge who had quoted, received or evaded it.

In the next section of this article, the writer informs us that it was the landlady of Robert's first lodgings in London who pointed him in the direction of the Baptist Chapel in *Romney Street* but, in his series of sketches called, 'Baptist Worthies,' Dr Landels assures us that it was not his landlady but a laundress who worked for the house. Be that as it may, the advice that he heeded was about to give his life an important new direction. The pastor of this chapel was the Rev Christopher Woollacott, a humble but highly esteemed minister who had already proved his potential by expanding his congregation at Modbury in Devon from a mere handful to over seventy and whose preachings had become renowned for their 'evangelical intensity.' Judging by the minister's account of his arrival in Westminster, I should imagine that any minister's preaching would have required a certain amount of vigour to be at all effective:

'On the first Lord's Day after our arrival, I was filled with horror at the dreadful exhibition of man's vilest passions which I saw when passing through Strutton's Ground and the Broadway. I had never beheld the like and had not imagined that human beings in a civilized country could be so lost to all sense of shame. There were no police then to restrain the dissolute by force, nor city missionaries to allure them by kindness to a holier path. I trembled for I feared that it would be impossible to preserve my children from contamination in the neighbourhood of such scenes…'

However, just as the Rev Woollacott had made his mark at Westminster for nine years, Robert had also made his on the minister's family. Despite the fact that his eldest daughter apparently had several other suitors, it was Robert who both attracted and held

Elizabeth's attention. 'She was but short in stature, with striking dark eyes, and he used to tell his children that he fell in love with those brown eyes then and there,' says Dorothy Pearce Gould, one of Robert and Elizabeth's granddaughters, in her charming little book *Diamonds in Drummond Street* reverently dedicated to her mother and grandmother. It was at this chapel that both Robert and Elizabeth were baptized by her father and the following extract is taken from a moving account by one of Elizabeth's relatives:

'On the way home from her father's preaching at Jewin Street Chapel, the Rev Woollacott remarked a soberness and seriousness in his daughter's manner and conversation which led him to hope that the Word might have been blessed to her. Some months after she communicated to him the joyful news that it was even so and that love to her Saviour led her to desire to be baptized and join herself to the Lord's Church. At the early age of under sixteen, her wishes in this respect were gratified. On coming before the Church as a candidate, her father asked her, 'Now, my dear, if I or the deacons should at any time see aught in your conduct that we thought inconsistent and we came and pointed it out to you, do you think you should take it kindly?' She replied, 'If the righteous smite me it shall be a kindness; an excellent oil that shall not break my head.' Her full heart now found vent in a flood of tears and not many left that meeting who did not weep with her who wept.'

When the minister resigned his post at Westminster in 1834 for a trial year at another beleaguered chapel in *Little Wild Street, Lincoln's Inn Fields*, Robert also transferred his congregational allegiance. But exactly when he moved into lodgings with the Woollacotts is not certain. The dates we do have are as follows: in 1834, the Woollacotts moved to *Little Wild Street*; on the 16th November, 1836, Robert entered himself as a student at *Gray's Inn*; and, on the 6th April, 1839, Robert married Elizabeth at *St Pancras Old Church*. Reade's account of Robert's activities compresses the sequence of events as follows:

'He was a Baptist and lodged with a Baptist minister and his two daughters. He fell in love with one of them, proposed to her and was accepted. The couple were married without pomp and, after the ceremony, the good minister took them aside and said, 'I have only £200 in the world; I have saved it a little at a time, for my two daughters. Here is your share, my children.' Then he gave his daughter £100 and she handed it to the bridegroom on the spot. The good minister smiled approval and they sat down to what fine folk call breakfast, but they called dinner, and it was.

After dinner and the usual ceremonies, the bridegroom rose and surprised them a little. He said, 'I am very sorry to leave you but I have a particular business to attend to; it will take me just one hour.' Of course there was a look or two interchanged, especially by every female there present, but the confidence in him was too great to be disturbed and this was his first eccentricity. He left them, went to Gray's Inn and put down his name as a student for the Bar. He then paid away his wife's dowry in the fees and returned within the hour. Next day the married clerk was at the office as usual and entered on a twofold life. He worked as a clerk till five, dined in the Hall of Gray's Inn as a sucking barrister and studied hard at night...'

However, despite this romantic compression, there are two major factors in Robert's life which the novelist has omitted and which I would like to include. The first is the fact that his parents had already emigrated to America. Under what circumstances and with how many children, we can not be sure but a census for New York some thirty years later lists the members of father Robert's family and the Blanchards from France living together as one household: Robert Lush; Lucy Foote; William Henry Lush, merchant; Harriet Emma Woollacott, his wife; Martha Durant and her two daughters, Lucy and Anne; and Susan Wickham, Robert's stepdaughter. You will notice from this list that Robert junior's brother, William Henry, had, by then, married Elizabeth's younger sister, Harriet Emma, so we might suppose that Robert was not the only youngster to stay in England at the time his parents emigrated. Furthermore, Dorothy Pearce Gould informs us that, after Robert's engagement to Elizabeth, he went out to visit his family in New York in order 'to discover what prospects the new country offered to young men. Fortunately for London, Robert disliked America. He returned to the metropolis and married Elizabeth.' And how different many of our lives would have been had he decided to settle across the water!

The second omission concerns the significance of the chapel in *Little Wild Street*. As I have already mentioned, the life of this chapel was not in a particularly healthy state when the Rev Woollacott accepted the position as its pastor. Its former pastor, Mr Hargreaves, had resigned leaving the church without a minister for nearly six years and the doors were even closed for a period between 1830 and 1831. For one of London's more notable churches, formed in 1691 shortly after the Spanish Ambassador had been evicted for not paying his debts by a mob which 'was not in a mood to make nice distinctions' and proud of its associations with Daniel Defoe, the author of Robinson Crusoe, Joseph Hughes, the founder of the *British and Foreign Bible Society*, John Thomas, the venerated colleague of William Carey in India, and John Howard, the celebrated prison philanthropist, there was clearly an urgent need to restore its ailing congregation. But the new pastor had already achieved one miracle in Devon and, judging by the number of people who attended the public meeting to commemorate his union with this church, it was clearly hoped that he might be able to perform another, which he did. The church community took on a new lease of life and quickly re-established itself as a distinguished centre of Nonconformist influence, promoting a second wave of philanthropy which was not common during the early days of the nineteenth century. Once again, under the leadership of the Rev Woollacott, together with the full support of his family, the church continued to be identified with exemplary work for bettering the conditions of the poor. And there can be little doubt that the mood of Christian fellowship that was nurtured by it made a deep impression on the newly married couple who would soon be in a position to alleviate the suffering of many hundreds of lost souls crowded into the wretched tenement houses between *Goodge Street* and *Euston Station*. However, before we move forward in time, this transcription of a newspaper report sheds a little more light on the magnanimous personality of Elizabeth's father:

'The pastor and his wife were out for a walk one evening when they noticed two men running towards them. Naturally, fearing a collision, the couple stepped aside but it was too late and they fell to the ground, considerably stunned and bruised. The pastor then seized one of the men by his trousers after which he and his wife were both kicked by the assailant in a most savage manner. The poor lady suffered severe bruising to her side while her husband suffered a sprained wrist and lacerated thumb and, had their screams not been heard by a patrolling policeman, their injuries might have been far worse. And, after the ensuing struggle with the policeman, the villain and his accomplice were both apprehended. When the matter finally reached the courts, it came as no surprise to hear the villains trying hard to excuse themselves by saying that they were drunk and had only intended to have a little fun. But what really surprised us all was the manner in which the pastor did his utmost to play down the incident. And, even when the judge sentenced Mr Slater to twenty-one days in the *House of Correction* and fined Mr Mountain sixty shillings, the pastor insisted that the penalties were too severe. Accordingly, Mr Mountain's sentence was changed to one month in prison with hard labour.'

Robert, Elizabeth and their children continued to support the church in *Little Wild Street* until Christopher Woollacott retired in 1863 and the chapel itself was only demolished in 1902, after a long and distinguished history, to clear the route for the new thoroughfare from Euston to the Strand.

Once they were married, the law student and his wife made their first home in Mecklenburg Square, not far from Lincoln's Inn Fields, and Reade gives us some idea of what a busy man Robert must have been:

'This (routine) was followed by a still stronger example of duplicate existence and one without a parallel in my reading and experience: he became a writer and produced a master-piece, which, as regarded the practice of our courts, became at once the manual of attorneys, counsel, and judges. The author, though his book was entitled 'Practice,' showed some qualities of a jurist and corrected soberly but firmly unscientific legislature and judicial blunders. So here was a student of Gray's Inn, supposed to be picking up in that Inn a small smattering of law, yet, to diversify his crude studies, instructing mature counsel and correcting the judges themselves at whose chambers he attended daily, cap in hand, as an attorney's clerk.

There's an intellectual hotch-potch for you! All this did not in his Inn qualify him to be a barrister but years and dinners did.

After some weary years he took the oaths at Westminster and vacated by that act his place in Bishop's office. He was a pauper – for an afternoon – but work that has been long and tediously prepared can be executed quickly and adverse circumstances, when Perseverance conquers them, can turn round and become an ally. The ex-clerk and young barrister had ploughed and sowed with such pains and labour that he reaped with comparative ease. Half the managing clerks in London knew him and believed in him. They had the ear of their employers and brought him pleadings to draw and motions to make. His book, too, brought him clients and he was soon in full career as a junior counsel and special pleader. Senior counsel too found that they could rely upon his zeal, accuracy, and learning. They began to request that he might be retained with them in difficult cases, and he became first junior counsel at the Bar; and so much for Perseverance...'

Even before Robert had published his famous book, referred to as 'Practice' in the above passage and which I shall describe in greater detail, he had already published his first book in 1838 entitled *The Act for the Abolition of Arrest on Mesne Process*. This was a book relating to arrest for bad debts and incorporated copious notes explaining the alterations in the law and how legal practice was consequently effected. According to one critic, 'It gave the greatest promise by its learning and by the evidence it afforded to the author's possessing the instincts of a sound critic on points of law...We find in this little text-book the student at Gray's Inn criticising with the greatest boldness and with apparent correctness the framing of the statute...' But, encouraged by this success, he then went on to publish his most famous work in 1840, barely a year after his marriage, *Practice of the Superior Courts of Common Law at Westminster in Actions and Proceedings over which they have a Common Jurisdiction*, otherwise simply known as *Lush's Practice*. And the critic continues: 'The time chosen was specially favourable for a new work on practice. The labours of the *Common Law Commission* appointed in 1834 had borne fruit in the introduction of several important reforms in the procedure of the Courts and no more lucid and capable interpreter could have appeared than Mr Lush.' This book received no less than three editions, the first being revised by James Stephen in 1855 and, ten years later by Joseph Dixon. It has been said that it should have received many more in line with its rival compilation, Chitty's *General Practice of the Law*, whose section on common law was edited by Robert himself in 1842, but, nonetheless, his own work heralded its author as one of the leading authorities on the laws of the time. Indeed, on account of this book alone, Robert Lush's name remained a household word in the homes of lawyers for many years to come and I was amused to discover, quite recently, that not only my own lawyer in Scotland could quote various phrases of its text but also that one of the current judges in our family found it necessary to refer one of his colleagues to it to clarify a point of law which hadn't changed since that time. How often do we hear that today's reference books are often out of date before they reach the bookshelves?

Whether or not Robert was assisted by his family associations with the Nonconformists is not certain, although I should imagine quite possibly. Nevertheless, he divided the lion's share of the best commercial business in the Guildhall with the future Chief Justice Bovill for many years and it was during this time that he accrued most of his wealth although he obviously had some trouble being seen on account of his size. Indeed, there is an amusing story about him being asked by the judge to stand on a stool so that he could be seen by the rest of the Court, to which he replied, 'Forgive me, your Lordship, but I am already am.' However, despite the fact that he was 'short in stature and not robust in appearance,' his mellow but penetrating voice managed to fill the Court without apparent effort and 'accorded well with his style of eloquence which was what Cicero calls the *temperatum genus loquendi.*' And, with his continuous application to intellectual labour of the severest kind, 'not only did he become an accomplished lawyer but, what was much rarer, a lawyer who had perfect command over his resources.' 'It was a part of his religion to do whatever he had to do well' and, judging by a report from one of the newspapers, it would appear that those whom he represented had little cause for complaint:

Sir Robert Lush

'It was only when I saw him near at hand, undistinguished by the wig, that I realised how fine a face he has.'

Lady Elizabeth Lush

'Her soft, musical voice was an index to her kindness of heart.'

'His clients can tell how thoroughly he made himself acquainted with the details of the cases entrusted to him and could never complain of his being indifferent to their interests whether the case was gained or lost.'

Meanwhile, back on the home front at *34, Mecklenburg Square*, Elizabeth was busy raising children. Their first child, Lucy Elizabeth, was born in 1840 and, sadly, died only fourteen months later but their next child, Robert Christopher, heralded the first of ten children who reached adulthood. Consequently, a growing family and shortage of space forced them to find more spacious accommodation and the 1851 census finds them living at *3, Gordon Square* together with three servants, including the nurse, Elizabeth West, who remained loyal to the family at least until the deaths of Robert and Elizabeth in 1881. (The 1881 census not only lists Elizabeth West as 61 and a former nurse but also, rather surprisingly, a certain Emma Lusher, a 27 year old kitchen maid residing with the family.) But it was the family's next move to *60, Avenue Road*, St John's Wood, in the mid 1850's that was to witness its extraordinary involvement with the church community and the poverty-stricken people of the district of the church.

Chapter Two

Sowing Seeds

Following the peak of the Evangelical Revival in 1815, there was a surge in new Nonconformist Churches that 'shared fully in the ecclesiastical prosperity of the Victorian era.' And, in 1852, Sir Morton Peto, the famous engineer responsible for building the railway line from the Crimean city seaport of Sevastopol to Balaklava, had the vision of turning the old *Diorama* in *Park Square East* into a chapel as he felt that there was an urgent need of Baptist witness in that neighbourhood. With the consent of the Commissioners of Woods and Forests, and the proviso that the original frontage would be preserved, this bold and most difficult engineering enterprise was carried out at a cost of £18,000, largely due to the generosity of Sir Morton himself. 1. Perhaps surprisingly, no initial allowance had been made for an organ and there was only limited accommodation for a small choir. It was only in 1858 that a powerful harmonium was provided and played by Mr Ebenezer Carr, this instrument eventually being replaced by a full-size organ. But, with a seating capacity of 1,500, a magnificent stone pulpit with alabaster panels and an enchanting vestibule with deep stone staircases, the building was ready for its first Divine Service on the 1st May, 1855.

The chapel's first minister was the Rev William Landels, who had come down to London from the *Circus Chapel* in Birmingham and was to minister at Regent's Park for the next twenty-eight years. It is interesting to note that, even when the church was actually formed in 1856, its membership already amounted to 192 but credit must be given to this popular and industrious minister for an increase to 545 members only four years later. The very fact that the *Baptist College* in Stepney moved to its new home in Regent's Park only months after the formation of the church must have also added a certain degree of vigour since the chapel then became the new spiritual home of its Principals, Dr Angus, Mr Roberts and Dr Gould, of their families and also of many of their students. As we shall see, these people were about to make a highly significant contribution to the life of the church and all that it encompassed. But, during the first Pastorate of the Rev Landels, as many as 2,000 names were enrolled as members so there can be little doubt that the choice of minister had been a wise one. The Rev William Brock of Hampstead tells us something about this remarkable man: 'I recall a figure slight and almost slim but firm and muscular, features strongly marked, a manner usually serious and reserved but often melting into a gracious smile. I have watched him being roped for an Alpine ascent or girding himself for intellectual adventure at Exeter Hall and there was the same look of self-possession and self-help. I used to hear him preach in those days and his style of preaching made a deep impression on us all. He spoke at that time from memory, never hesitating to go back along his sentences for a word lost or misplaced; and this habit would have given an artificial tone to his address but for the substantial stuff that was in them and the subdued and unmistakable intensity of the man himself. The accent of conviction was always there.' And there can be little doubt that he was also a popular choice not only for preaching opening and anniversary sermons in various Baptist chapels but also for participating in services of other denominations in London theatres and, under the auspices of that staunch Evangelical, Lord Shaftesbury, in *St James' Hall*. His voice was constantly heard at meetings of the *London City Mission*, the *British and Foreign Bible Society* and other missionary societies and, in 1876, he was called to the chair of the *Baptist Union* where he was devoted to the formation of the *Annuity Fund* for retired Baptist ministers. Therefore, not surprisingly, a presentation was made to him on his retirement on behalf of over five hundred ministers testifying to the high esteem in which he was held.

Also, on the 6th January, 1856, the Sunday School was opened in a large room under the chapel and, between the years 1874 and 1880, there were no less than 1,168 members with an average attendance of 858. And a Junior Room was opened in 1857, closely followed by an Infants' Classroom. The scholars of these schools took part in the *Sunday School Union Exams* and in the *International Bible-Reading Association*. It is perhaps worth pointing out here that the concept of Sunday Schools had only been born some fifty years earlier at Gloucester and Forster's great social landmark, the *Education Act*,

Regent's Park Chapel, London

'A church on fire with the true missionary spirit.'

which provided education for all, was not passed until 1870. So, in between times, the Church played a vital role in the education of children, for whom certain protective measures had already been incorporated by the *Factory Act* of 1833 and by Lord Shaftesbury's *Mines Act* of 1842 and for whom the proof of a new wave of sympathy was going to manifest itself in Lewis Carroll's *Alice in Wonderland* in 1865. Although the Victorian maxim, 'Children should be seen and not heard,' does not court much popularity nowadays, we must not forget that, prior to the *Mines Act*, Shaftesbury had discovered boys as young as four working down the mines where they would have barely been seen.

According to Dorothy Pearce Gould, the new church was 'full of the warmth of fellowship and real family life where the keynote of preaching was the Gospel in all its fullness. *Regent's Park Chapel* was always a church on fire with the true missionary spirit, not content to sit back at ease but always breaking out into new ways of service, putting first things first, winning souls for Christ, and building up young lives in His Service.' All the same, the matter of membership was not to be taken lightly, according to J.H.Shakespeare:

'The rules for Church Membership were very strict. Each candidate was interviewed by two Elders after being recommended by the Pastor, and, if considered satisfactory, was nominated at the Church Meeting, accepted the following month, baptised the Wednesday after and received at the Communion service the following Sunday Evening. The wife of the chapel-keeper, attired in a light grey linsey dress with cape to the waist, white cap with frills, and tied with white ribbon under the chin and white gloves, officiated at all Baptisms, Weddings and other functions and magnified her office in every way, always speaking of 'Our Church' in a respectful and dignified manner, and thus keeping the *younger* members in wholesome awe!'

Such was the church that welcomed Robert and his family into its fold. All its work among the poor, the sick, the sad and the sorrowful was incorporated in the *Domestic Mission* and it was into this, especially, that Elizabeth threw her heart and soul. She was no mere figurehead in Christian life, taking her full share in the life of her Church, serving on many committees and becoming one of the early pioneers of the *Zenana Mission* which I will describe in greater detail later in the chapter. And there can be little doubt that she had been strongly influenced by the good work of her parents while still a child. Besides her father's ministry, to which I have already drawn attention, her mother, also Elizabeth Ann, used to teach at the *Sabbath School* in Modbury, formed a female Prayer Meeting and was an active collector for the *Bible Society*. All this, together with the happiness of her own married life, the love of her children and her warm-hearted nature made her quick to sympathise with those in trouble and eager to share her blessings with those who were much less fortunate. As Dorothy mentions:

'It was usual for the Lush family to drive to Regent's Park Chapel in the carriage and pair round the park by the zoo. But surely, sometimes, they must have driven the alternative way outside the park and down Albany Street where the little streets run down towards Hampstead Road? And did she not catch glimpses of women, careworn, weary, hearing evidence of poverty, ignorance and sin? Yes, indeed, and of little children clothed in rags, playing in the gutters, roaming the streets with nowhere to go and no one to care for them…Did not these faces haunt her when she went home to her own happy family? These were the people for whom the Domestic Mission existed but how many of them ever crossed the threshold of the church? How were they to be reached, taught, helped and made aware that they were born to be the Children of God?'

Inspired by the work of Mrs Ranyard, who was training Christian women to nurse the sick in their own homes at about this time, and also, most probably, by the work of Florence Nightingale – let us not forget that the youngest daughter born to the Lushes in 1857 was called Florence only a year after the Crimean War – Elizabeth was determined to start her own 'Cottage Meeting,' as it was then called. But the first task was to find a suitable venue. She knew that they would not voluntarily enter a church so she had to find a location where they would feel at ease and the first place she found was a small room behind a grocer's shop in what is now *William Road*. The room was only equipped with the basic essentials but Wednesday afternoon was chosen for the meeting thereby starting a tradition with barely a score of mothers which lasted for the next hundred years. How Elizabeth initially gathered her flock is not known although she was certainly bold and determined enough to have toured the squalid, if not dangerous, streets and invited them herself. A few years later, she was certainly stopped by a policeman who tried to dissuade her, for the good of her own safety, from visiting someone living in a street of ill repute and she simply answered, 'But I am going to see my friends. Why should I have anything to fear?' And not once did she consider herself to be in any kind of danger.

But whatever steps were taken to recruit these women in the first place evidently paid off because they came and came again. Week after week, in that one little room, they found a true friend, a family woman with a loving heart and one who had already experienced the trauma of a lost child. As Dr Landels describes in his book, *Baptist Worthies*,

'How she sympathised with them in their troubles! How unwilling to give them up even after they had repeatedly disappointed her hopes! What interest she took in them! What joy she took in their joy!'

and as Dorothy describes in hers:

'She read the Bible and very simply explained its meaning. She sang hymns to them and taught them to sing, word by word, line by line, for they could not read. She prayed with them and taught them to pray. She visited them in their homes and, somehow, always left the impression that she was honoured by doing so. The Cottage Meeting grew and, before long, it was impossible to squeeze another mother into the little room. What should they do?'

As it happened, Robert became a QC and bencher of *Gray's Inn* in 1857 and Treasurer of that Inn in 1860. Not only was he rising steadily in his profession with the rewards that his status commanded but he was already gaining influence in the Church. From the 9th November, 1858, he was Treasurer of the *Baptist Fund* and subsequent clerical roles included his being President of the *Sunday School Union*, Vice-President of the *Evangelical Alliance* and an Elder of *Regent's Park Chapel*. And just as Elizabeth had always supported him, 'She took an intellectual interest in his preparatory studies, helped him in correcting the proofs of the books which first brought him into notice and, by her cheerful buoyant spirit, greatly encouraged him in his work...Especially was she ready to encourage him in the liberal and generous acts to which he was naturally inclined,' so was he always inclined to support her. Ever since his student days, Robert had given away at least a tenth of his income to various funds. He was also a generous friend and relative – some even thought him over-generous – and the more he earned, the more he gave. (One of his donations to *Gray's Inn* at about this time included a pair of George III wine coasters engraved with the crest and inscribed 'The Gift of Robert Lush, 1860.') So when he saw the dilemma faced by his wife over inadequate premises for her Cottage Meetings, despite the fact that two larger rooms had been provided, it will come as no surprise that he felt fully inclined to help her out.

The story handed down to us describes how, on the occasion of a special anniversary, perhaps that of their twenty-fifth wedding anniversary, Robert wanted to give his wife a special present. Retrospectively, Dr Landels pointed out that 'she might well have spent the money on herself as a personal gift or adornment, such as society would have thought becoming to one in her station, a gift which would have become an heirloom in the family and which, therefore, some of the members of the family might have liked her to accept for their sakes as well as her own.' But I suspect that Robert knew well enough what she would have preferred to an adornment such as a diamond necklace. Indeed, what she was crying out for was a hall large enough to cater not only for an army of some four hundred women but also for their husbands and children as well. The Gospel was not confined to poor mothers! So, in 1864, a year before Robert succeeded Mr Justice Crompton at the Queen's Bench, plans were drafted for a *Mission Hall* in *Charles Street* (later named *Drummond Street*) which Elizabeth often referred to as her 'diamond necklace' for she knew that 'men, women and little children were of far greater worth than diamonds and that, one day, they would shine in the Kingdom of God with a far greater brilliance.' And not only was there to be a hall but also a three-storied building of flats, each equipped with a sink, a lavatory, running water and gas where some of the women, mostly widows, could end their days in relative decency. There was even a flat roof where they could dry their washing! The flats were known as *Lush's Buildings* and were considerably in advance of their times. As Dorothy explains, 'The plan was to offer these flats at a very nominal rent in order to help the very neediest. The missionary (attached to *Regent's Park Chapel*) gladly undertook to collect the nominal rents and keep a friendly eye on the inhabitants and these rents would be put aside by the landlord for the upkeep of the Mission Hall and the flats.' And it would appear that this plan was successfully carried through to at least the first decades of the next century after which matters became more complicated with another surge of housing reform. However, it wasn't until the 1970's that these buildings were finally demolished for redevelopment and, as we shall see, their purpose certainly lived up to their benefactors' expectations.

Despite a most untimely snowstorm, the *Mission Hall* was opened in January, 1865, with a well-attended public meeting presided over by Dr Landels and the scene was set for a huge growth in Christian work. A *Father's Class* was started by Elizabeth herself, fully determined to teach those 'rough men the Word of God' and the following anecdote gives an indication of her winning ways even with them:

'A woman had come to Elizabeth in dire straits. Her husband was a fine specimen of a man but morally weak and wayward. He had served in the army during the Crimean War and his soldier's life had produced bad habits, the worst of which was his intemperance which forced his family to live in great poverty and distress. Now Elizabeth confronted the soldier and implored him to relinquish his drinking upon which he reminded her that him drinking beer was, on the face of it, no worse than her drinking wine. She therefore asked him if he would give up beer if she gave up wine, even though she believed that a certain amount of wine was beneficial for her health. He promised that he would so the deal was struck. However, when they met a few weeks later, the soldier was troubled by what he saw. Elizabeth was looking pale and fragile and, concerned that her abstinence was at the root of her ill health, he said that one of them would have to break the agreement so she could recover. Consequently, it was Elizabeth who resumed her daily intake of wine but the strategy had worked because the soldier stuck to his new way of life and his family began to flourish.'

A Monday class was also added to the original Wednesday meeting with the assistance of the daughters of Dr Angus and activities such as the *Penny Bank*, the *Men's Slate Club* and the *Band of Hope* were all taken on board to encourage the people to follow a more Christian way of life. And I should imagine that the first tenants of the flats, in particular, regarded their windfall as manna from Heaven.

Lush's Buildings in *Drummond Street*, London

Elizabeth's 'diamond necklace.'

As I say, Robert was promoted to the Queen's Bench that year and was knighted at Windsor Castle on the 20th November. In the wake of such a promotion, it was customary for the new judge to throw a party at his Inn and, at Robert's, it is said that, as he was not particularly adept at selecting entertainment, one of his colleagues suggested an *ad hoc* performance of arias and choruses from *La Traviata* which, I daresay, must have been quite amusing. However, in the true tradition of a Baptist pastor's family at the time, Elizabeth's mother stoutly declared, 'I care but little for the honours accorded him by man in comparison with those which God has conferred on him. He and our daughter are Children of God, the highest title, and they will, by and by, occupy a seat at His right Hand which is the greatest honour!' But, whatever the Rev Woollacott and his wife thought of the accolade, or, for that matter, *La Traviata*, there could be little doubt that Robert's new influential capacity would be of even greater service to the Church and its Missions.

Essentially a man of peace who preferred 'a pleasing solitariness to a sea of noises and hoarse disputes,' Robert had never cast an election vote in his life and comments in the press suggested that both his non-political views and religious ideals may have hindered his professional progress. Certainly, the latter assumption was easily dismissed by him and it might be worth pointing out that his great friend, Mr Justice Shee, the first Catholic judge in England since the Reformation, was not refused a judgeship on account of his religious convictions and neither were Lords Hatherley and Selborne because of theirs. And, as far as politics was concerned, Robert had by no means set a precedent. As the *Solicitor's Journal* reports:

'The appointment will give unqualified satisfaction to the profession. Mr Lush has never sat in Parliament and, in choosing a judge from without the narrow circle of Parliamentary lawyers, the Lord Chancellor has followed an excellent precedent established some years ago by himself.'

All the same, by accepting this judgeship, Robert had also resigned himself to a substantial fall in income. The money in the legal profession was made at the Bar, not at the Bench, and, by all accounts, his barrister's practice had been very successful. Nevertheless, despite his liberal generosity, his Will reveals a very tidy system of investments and the 1861 census shows a contingent of no less than six servants, subsequently increased to seven by 1881. These are listed as: Elizabeth, 26, nursemaid, James Davis, 35, butler, Elizabeth West, 40, (the ever faithful) nurse, Sarah Watson, 37, cook, Ann Rye, 44, housemaid, and David Shepherd, 16, page. We also know that both Robert and Elizabeth had their own private carriages and that their house was equipped not only with a conservatory but with a garden large enough to contain a tennis court and croquet lawn as well as a paddock for the cow and, presumably, the horses. So it would seem that, by this time, a fall in income was not going to drastically affect the family's circumstances in *Avenue Road*. Perhaps, even more importantly, it wasn't going to affect the impact of their Christian philanthropy either. As far as the *Domestic Mission* was concerned, two of the highlights of the neighbourhood calendar were undoubtedly the winter tea-party at *Regent's Park Chapel* and the summer one in the garden at *Avenue Road*, both paid for by Robert and Elizabeth. This biblical quotation, 'When thou makest a feast, call the poor, the maimed, the lame, the blind; and thou shalt be blessed,' must have been ringing in their ears because as many as four hundred mothers were invited to these parties and Dorothy clearly recalls her mother, Florence, describing the huge joints of beef and ham that were served and the massive tent erected in the paddock. 'One year,' she says, 'the sun forgot to shine and a sudden thunderstorm broke. Without any hesitation, Lady Lush threw open her house to the whole party and mother remembered how it swarmed with women upstairs and down!'

In addition to these events, Elizabeth's personal diaries, written between 1865 and 1867 also reveal an extremely busy social schedule at home. To describe her as naturally warm-hearted, loving and gregarious would probably be a gross understatement of this remarkable woman but, apart from regular guests like Drs Landels and Angus, and Justices Shee, Bovill, Thesiger and Cockburn and their families, there were obviously many other influential people who may have shown a supportive interest in her Christian work. The following extract taken from the *Christian Secretary*, Connecticut, describes two visits made by American Baptists to

Avenue Road either side of Robert's promotion:

'In London in 1859, Dr Landels invited us to breakfast with him. When the time arrived, it was Lady Lush's carriage that called for us and in it were her parents, the Rev Christopher Woollacott and his wife, very pleasant people. The breakfast, for some reason, was at Justice Lush's house; he was absent but Lady Lush received us very cordially and the occasion was much enjoyed. The family was a delightful one and there was quite a number of children with at least five daughters, some of whom were quite young and with whom we played graces on the fine lawn at the rear of the mansion. Again in London, on a Sunday evening some thirteen years later at Dr Landels' Chapel, Lady Lush recognised us and most cordially invited us and Dr Graves, who was with us, to dine at her house on the following Thursday. There we found Dr Landels and other friends and the feast was charming in all respects. Of the five daughters, only the youngest was at home, the others having married with homes of their own. After dinner, Lady Lush took us out to the lawn, showing how it had been enlarged and improved and how grounds beyond had been added where they kept and pastured a cow, a rare thing in those pleasant suburbs of that great city. Delightful is the memory of our visits to this noble Christian home...'

and as Dr Landels points out in *Baptist Worthies*:

'To almost every needy and deserving object she was ready to lend a helping hand...For orphanages and missions, she toiled indefatigably. Aged Pilgrims and Incurables found in her a sympathising and energetic friend.' And she was unquestionably very persuasive: 'She could speak more winningly than most for her soft, musical voice was an index to her kindness of heart.'

But, besides her work with the Church and *Mission Hall*, Elizabeth was also actively involved with the *Orphan Working School* at Haverstock Hill and the Baptist *Zenana Mission*, both of which required liberal funding. Many an orphan had cause to be grateful for the huge work she did on his or her behalf but the *Zenana Mission*, of which she was not only one of the first pioneers but also the first treasurer, a position she held until the time of her death, cast its net far beyond the realms of Regent's Park to countries such as China, Italy, Norway and India. The aim of this Mission was to send out trained women missionaries to visit and nurse the sick in their own homes and, of course, to teach them the Gospel. To give some idea of the extent of the Mission's influence in this field, by 1881 there were more than twenty European teachers and almost fifty native teachers who regularly visited five hundred *Zenanas* and instructed over a thousand native families in India alone. Robert was not known for lengthy speeches, either in or out of Court, although he had acquired a reputation for sticking to the point, an art which most of his fellow Justices apparently lacked, but the following quotation from one of them gives us a valuable insight into his views on women, the Mission and the Empire:

'In India, women are more degraded than in any other part of the globe, Africa excepted. In Indian society, at the present day, women are subject to so many indignities that they may be said to have a great claim upon us. We, in England, owe much to woman's influence and we can not tell what will be the results of the efforts put forth to grapple with India through the education of ladies there. Ordinary civilisation will not win India for Christ; it must be gained through the mothers of India....In this country, we know little more of India than that it is a great nation, consisting of more than two hundred millions of population and we do not possess it merely for commercial purposes but that, throughout the length and breadth of it, we may make felt the power and glory and greatness of the Gospel.'

And to give some idea of how Elizabeth appealed for funds to finance the operation, here is a letter written by her on black-edged paper in 1880 when she was already suffering from a terminal illness and had only recently lost her son, Samuel Clarence:

'The Ladies Association for the support of Zenana Work and Bible Women in India and China in connection with the Baptist Missionary Society.

My dear Friend,

May I present an appeal to you on behalf of our Zenana Mission, first because we need help to complete our Calcutta Home and normal schools; second, because we require special annual subscriptions for our Bible Women in China; third, because our present income is inadequate to the expenditure to which we are already committed and we need more annual subscribers. In addition to these things, new doors are constantly opening and new agents are offering themselves for the work. On these grounds may I earnestly ask you to contribute towards the necessary funds that we may take up all the work that our hands find to do? It is about twenty years since the wife of one of our missionaries first thought of gaining admission to the Zenanas and, after several attempts, eventually succeeded. Thus, a Baptist was the first to take the word of life to the women, as Carey had formerly taken it to the men of India. This effort was succeeded by other work and now most Denominations have their Zenana Societies. But I am pleading for our own and ask for a liberal response. Ought not we who daily pray, 'Thy Kingdom come" to be able to say, Lord, thou knowest that I am doing all I can to help its coming.

That he may enable each one of us not only to say but to do is the prayer of

yours faithfully,

Elizabeth A. Lush (treasurer)

PS
Since the above was written, a Lady has sent us £210 for outfit, passage money and one year's income for one of our lady agents and promises to pay £140 annually for her life.

Hon. Secretaries:
Mrs Angus, The College, Regent's Park
Mrs Smith, Highbury.'

It can be no surprise that she was Treasurer of this society for so long since those meetings which she chaired usually raised a great deal of money. At one such meeting in 1878, no less than £400 was raised which, as you will have noticed from the letter, will have been sufficient to have sent two agents to India for a whole year. Nor can it be a surprise that both Robert and Elizabeth's efforts in this direction were highly commended: 'It is only due to both to say that they have awakened an interest in this branch of missionary enterprise which, year by year, promises yet more successfully to extend the knowledge of the Gospel throughout our Indian Empire.

In Dorothy Pearce Gould's book, written in the 1950's, she says, 'In this swiftly-moving, mechanical age, we are apt to think that our grandparents lived a quiet, untroubled existence with long hours of leisure. Yet, when one considers the facts, their lives must have been full and busy.' As we shall soon see, if touring the country on Circuit wasn't enough to keep Robert busy, his judicial qualities were about to earn him a seat on two radical Royal Commissions. And, as far as Elizabeth was concerned, the notion of a Victorian lady trying to alleviate her boredom by weaving a tapestry or standing around with a paintbrush couldn't have been further from the truth. On top of all her Christian commitments, she had a large household with six servants to supervise and, as time went on, a great deal of entertaining to do. Nowadays, the prospect of hosting a weekly dinner party for six may seem like something of an ordeal but, as these fragments from her social diaries reveal, Elizabeth's schedule was awesome, with or without staff:

1865

Feb 14th: dinner (14)
Feb 16th: dinner (20)
Feb 21st: evening party (31 ladies, 28 gents)

1867

Feb 14th: party at home (79)
Feb 18th: dinner (18)

June 4th: children to Mrs Vaughan's 6pm
June 5th: Lady Malins at home
June 6th: Mrs Bliss dinner 7.30
June 7th: Mrs Marshman dinner 7.45
June 8th: Mrs Chambers dinner 7.30
June 11th: Merchant Taylors dinner 6pm
June 12th: Gray's Inn dinner 6.30
June 13th: dinner at home 7.30
June 14th: Lord Westminster dinner 7.45
June 15th: Mr Justice Montagu Smith dinner 7.45
June 20th: Church party at home (44)
        Dinner at home (20)

1868

Jan 18th: party (21 ladies, 33 gents)
Feb 11th: Gospel Mission in Italy (200)
June 16th: Juvenile party (44)

1869

Dec 31st: New Year's Eve party at Mission Hall 6pm (80)

The staff were probably relieved not to find any entries for Sundays or Mondays! However, with a family of seven at home, there still can't have been much respite. During the mid to late 1860's, in addition to Robert and Elizabeth, they would have had to cater for the needs of Mary, Caroline, Florence and Percy, and 'Montie' when he wasn't at *Westminster School*. More will be said about their careers and marriages later on but this would seem to be an opportune moment to mention the rest of the contingent as their progress would have been particularly relevant to the lives of Robert and Elizabeth at this time. Their eldest son, Robert Christopher, had entered *Trinity College*, Cambridge, in 1859 and been admitted to *Gray's Inn* in 1863. (It is worth pointing out that he was the only son to attend *Trinity College* whereas Herbert and Montie both attended *Trinity Hall*.) How he faired as an advocate is not clear but, in 1865, he married Alice Free, daughter of Colonel John Free of the *10th*

Bengal Cavalry and *East India Army*, and they had two children, Robert in 1866 and Alice a year later. Francis, their eldest daughter, had also married the Rev Hanmer Webb Peploe in 1863 and, by him, had three children, Frank, Howard and a daughter. Hanmer's father, John Birch Webb, was vicar of Weobly, Hereford, and his mother, Annie Peploe, was a prolific novelist with an output of over twenty-five titles including *Oliver Wyndham*, published in 1867, and the *Martyrs of Carthage*, twice published in 1850 and 1857. Herbert had just matriculated at *Trinity Hall* and was about to be admitted to the *Inner Temple* and his younger brother, Samuel Clarence, had just left *Westminster School* also destined for a legal career. But the family affair that must have surely attracted the most attention was the marriage between Robert's daughter, Elizabeth, and Charles Watkin Williams in 1865 not only because Watkin was eighteen years Elizabeth's senior and had been a widower for barely a year with several children to his credit but also because of a career that had switched from medicine to law and had already shown a strong leaning towards politics.

****

Charles Watkin Williams was born in 1828 at Llangar, Merionethshire. He was the eldest son of Peter Williams, rector of Llansannan, and, after being educated at *Ruthin Grammar School*, studied medicine under Erichsen at *University College Hospital* where he won the gold medal for comparative anatomy. For a time, he acted as house-surgeon before deciding to abandon medicine in London for law at Oxford where he matriculated in 1851. However, finding the accommodation at Oxford uncongenial, he never graduated and returned to London to enter the *Middle Temple*. There, he read law in the chambers of the renowned special pleader, Horatio Lloyd, and, presumably for some light relief, published *An Essay upon the Philosophy of Evidence, with a Discussion concerning the Belief in Clairvoyance* in 1853, followed by a second edition in 1855. However, despite his talent for writing, he pursued his official studies and was called to the Bar in 1854. Then, there is an interesting parallel with Robert's career because, in 1857, he published *An Introduction to the Principles and Practice of Pleading in Civil Actions in the Supreme Courts of Law at Westminster* which also established his reputation and brought him a large practice. He then married Henrietta Carey, daughter of William Henry Carey and niece of Vice-Chancellor Malins, and worked on both the Home and South-Eastern Circuits. According to the *Saturday Review*, 'He seldom led and relied upon logicality and clearness of statement rather than upon rhetoric or declamation but he was remarkable for a certain dry humour and was quite indifferent to hostile criticism.' In November, 1868, he entered Parliament as Liberal member for the Denbigh boroughs and sat for that constituency until 1880 when he was elected for Carnarvonshire.

As early as 1854, Watkin had published a pamphlet on the *Law of Church Rates* but, regardless of his Christian convictions, moved a resolution in the *House of Commons* on the 24th May, 1870 in favour of the disestablishment of the Church in Wales. Apparently, his speech displayed considerable knowledge of ecclesiastical history but the motion was opposed by Gladstone and lost by 164 votes. In 1873, he took silk, specialising in financial and mercantile cases such as *Thomas v the Queen* in 1874 and *Anderson v Morice* in 1876. In the former, Mr Thomas had invented a system of heavy rifled artillery which he then passed on to the Secretary of War without being adequately remunerated for his efforts and the latter concerned an insurance claim over a shipment of rice from Rangoon, part of which had found its way to the ocean floor when the ship sank. In 1875, he served on Sir Henry James's *Committee on Foreign Loans* but, on Gladstone's return to office in 1880, declined the post of Judge Advocate General offered to him by the Prime Minister, though, apparently, he would have been willing enough to have accepted the post of Solicitor General! And when Robert was promoted to the *Court of Appeal* in November of that year, Watkin was appointed to the vacant puisne judgeship, having recently declared that he would never accept such an office. This amusing translation from the Welsh appeared in the *St James's Gazette*:

'My constituents, they say I may forget you
For a seat upon the Bench. I answer, Fudge;
Let not idle fears of losing me beset you;
I will never be an ordinary Judge.

A place that may be good enough for Bramwell,
For Blackburn, and for Blackstone, I don't grudge
To the gentlemen who Law Reports can cram well;
But I'll not be an ordinary Judge.

The Exchequer, were it offered, I might think of;
But 't would be a derogation, should I budge
From the seat that you have given me, and slink off
In the ermine of an ordinary Judge.

So I talked, until there came a certain letter
From the Chancellor. This morning, with a nudge,
Whispered Cockburn, 'Brother Watkin, you had better
Bow to fate, and be an ordinary Judge."

It is also said that, although his constituents were reluctant to let him go, 'with considerate kindness, they gave him the help he wanted and pushed their coy member into a judgeship.' And I wonder what Robert had to say about the matter. We know that Robert had little time for politics and I think it is fair to assume that he would have liked to have been succeeded by his son-in-law so long as Watkin had made provisions for his drop in income, and for his family, just as he had done.

As a judge, Watkin was considered to be 'painstaking, fair and independent' and, in *nisi prius* business, 'his knowledge and quickness of apprehension were invaluable' even if some of his judgements in complicated cases were, at times, 'diffuse and loosely reasoned.' Some of his more noteworthy cases included *Sanders v Richardson* and *Munster v Lamb* but, perhaps, the most significant was that of the *Queen v Most* in 1881. This last case concerned Johann Most who had been indicted on twelve counts for publishing an article in his newspaper *Freiheit* which commended the murder of the Emperor of Russia, Alexander II, as an example to worldwide revolutionaries. It was also seen as a vicious attempt to create discord between the Queen and other sovereigns and was, therefore, taken very seriously. However, in this case, at least, Watkin's judgement was far from 'diffuse and loosely reasoned' – he agreed most clearly with the jury's verdict of guilty in less than fifty words.

He also submitted a paper to the *Council of Judges* advocating the abolition of distinctions between the common pleas and exchequer divisions but the retention of the chiefships and publicly repudiated their decisions announced in November, 1881, declaring that nothing less than an Act of Parliament should ever induce him to deprive a prisoner of the right of making a statement to a jury of facts not given in evidence. However, on the night of the 17th July, 1884, Watkin suffered a fatal heart attack while on circuit in Nottingham. The exact cause of his death has never been in doubt but questions have been raised about the circumstances. Suffice it to say that the first woman on the scene was not his poor wife, Elizabeth.

****

In the meantime, the 1870's witnessed a certain amount of legal activity that did bring Robert more into the public domain whether he intended to be there or not. The following extract from the *Christian Herald* describes one such example:

'Never shall we forget a scene we personally witnessed some ten years ago in which the late lamented judge took a leading part. It was on the occasion of the trial, at the Spring Assizes of 1871, of one who was found guilty of wilful murder in connection with a burglary which had been committed at Stratford, near London. The prisoner was most ably defended by Mr Montague Williams who exhausted all the resources of ingenuity and forensic skill in his eloquent appeal to the jury. The summing up of the judge, which was a masterpiece of lucid statement and legal exposition, made it abundantly clear that only one verdict could be returned and that of guilty. In a hush of breathless silence that solemn word was pronounced by the foreman of the jury and then followed a scene seldom witnessed in a court of justice. After a confession of guilt by the prisoner, the judge put on the black cap and addressed him in words which for intense earnestness and overwhelming pathos could scarcely have been exceeded. Having dwelt on the awful crime for which the prisoner stood condemned, Lord Justice Lush, then Sir Robert, in a few weighty words presented the great offer of salvation held out in the Gospel and concluded by quoting with tremulous voice and thrilling tone the words : 'The blood of Jesus Christ His

Son cleanseth us from all sin.' This exhortation to repentance and faith drew from the prisoner a hearty 'Amen,' which, there was at least every reason to believe, came from a soul really humbled and penitent before God. The scene is illustrated in one of the panels of our frontispiece.'

However, although Montie subsequently knotched up as many as a dozen distinctly more famous cases during the course of his career, Robert's next major case was perhaps one of the most sensational of all time to be brought before the English Court. Moreover, on a recent visit to *Gray's Inn*, I couldn't help noticing that the subject matter for the majority of sardonic cartoons on its walls was this particular case. It was the trial of the Tichborne Claimant in 1873 which not only lasted a full year but also attracted so much controversy and ill-feeling that Robert and his colleagues, Cockburn and Mellor, had to be given police protection. Indeed, such was the national interest in this case, I know of at least six publications relating to it produced between the years 1874 and 1913 and, no doubt, there were many more. *The Tichborne Romance* alone, by A. Steinmedz of the *Middle Temple*, sold 10,000 copies at 1s apiece between the Civil and Criminal trials and it is very clear that, despite the official verdict, not only was public opinion equally divided as to who the Claimant actually was but he himself seemed to be just as confused: in *The Tichborne Mystery*, Edward Priestman argues that the Claimant was a lunatic called Cresswell; in a multitude of works, Guildford Onslow shows how utterly convinced he was that the Claimant was, in fact, Sir Roger Tichborne; and, in July 1895, a confession by the Claimant swearing that he was not Sir Roger Tichborne but Arthur Orton was first published then repudiated!

In a nutshell, the story of the Tichborne Claimant went something like this. Sir Roger Tichborne was born into a prominent Catholic family in 1829 and educated at *Stonyhurst College* though, it would seem, not for very long. On leaving this college, he was then sent to Paris and, after returning to England, obtained a commission in the *Sixth Dragoon Guards* where he remained until 1853. His spirit of adventure then took him off to Rio de Janeiro the following year but, after awhile, he decided to return to England and secured a berth to Liverpool on a ship called the *Bella*. As it happened, this ship then ran into trouble and was wrecked but, although the rest of his family were certain that he had perished along with the other passengers and crew, his mother was so convinced that he had been rescued, she even placed advertisements in numerous newspapers in an attempt to find her son. At this point, however, the evidence given both by the Claimant and witnesses began to flounder. If, indeed, the Claimant had been rescued by another vessel and landed in Australia, presumably with one or two other shipmates, it couldn't be fathomed why he hadn't followed his original plan and made an immediate return to England as opposed to living a life of considerable hardship, taking on a barely educated wife and eking out a living as a butcher in remote village called Wagga Wagga, hardly much of a life for the son of a baronet. Then, in 1865, the father of Sir Roger died and it was about this time that the Claimant made his way back to England having, apparently, borrowed funds for the journey. Exactly why he chose such a circuitous route home was also unclear and he didn't reach London until Christmas Day, 1866. But, when he arrived, his first mission was not to visit Lady Tichborne, as one might have expected, but to seek out the family of another butcher named Orton claiming that this was the name of one of his associates in Australia. So this is where a muddle over the name, Arthur Orton, began.

Now the Claimant's original solicitor, a man named Holmes, was certainly inclined to believe his story but, before further committing himself to the case, suggested that his client might be interviewed by Lady Tichborne. His client readily consented and the meeting was duly arranged in a Parisian hotel. When the time came, it was alleged that the Claimant was ill in bed and did his utmost to prevent her from getting a close look at him but this was subsequently denied and Lady Tichborne acknowledged the man as her lost son with the highly convincing, and touching, words, 'How can a mother be mistaken in her son?' However, Lady Tichborne's recognition served little purpose as she died before the case came to court and, to make matters worse, Sir Roger's sweetheart denied that she had ever met the so-called Claimant as did the remainder of Roger's family, despite the fact that they had recognised certain tattoo marks on one of the Claimant's arms which bore an uncanny resemblance to those on the arm of Sir Roger.

Proceedings were first commenced at the Civil Trial in the *Court of Common Pleas*, presided over by Robert's friend and colleague, Chief Justice Bovill, and the Claimant was subsequently bailed much to the delight of a lively band of supporters who 'accompanied him down *Parliament Street*, shouting and cheering.' The matter had already caught the public eye and there can be little doubt that many people thought that the poor man was being robbed of what was rightfully his. Nevertheless, the Claimant lost his case and was then brought to the *Criminal Court*, presided over by Sir Alexander Cockburn, for perjury and forgery in supporting his claim to the Tichborne estates and, despite Robert's reputation for impartiality and fairness, the odds were stacked against the plaintiff from the outset. There had already been a great deal of publicity against the Claimant before the trial, fuelled by the personal views of the Lord Chief Justice; the formidable cross-examiner was Sir Henry Hawkins who led for the Crown and was about to conduct 'one of the most brilliant cross-examinations of all time'; his defence was entrusted to Dr Kenealy, a fine but eccentric scholar of the day who 'exhibited every fault incident to advocacy by insulting the judges, disgusting the jury and, finally, committing the cardinal blunder of undertaking to prove what was not really in issue, namely, that his client was in truth Sir Roger Tichborne'; and, although many key witnesses failed to testify, many of those who did were found to be wholly unreliable. Consequently, the Claimant, Thomas Castro, alias Arthur Orton, alias Sir Roger Tichborne, was sentenced to fourteen years penal servitude on the 28th February, 1874 and I close this summary with the following comment from Douglas Woodruff's book, *A Victorian Mystery*:

'The great doubt still hangs suspended. Probably for ever now, its key long since lost amid the irresponsible lawlessness, deception and transient aliases, and the homicides, of the mid-Victorian Australian bush, a mystery remains; and the strange enigma of the man who lost himself still walks in history with no other name than that which the common voice of his day accorded him: the Claimant.'

Interestingly, four years later in 1878, Robert dissented from the opinion of his two colleagues in the Tichborne trial in the case of *Martin v Mackonochie*. He held that a writ of prohibition ought not to be issued to Lord Penzance in respect of the second admonition of Mr Mackonochie, a view upheld by the majority of the *Court of Appeal* and later by the *House of Lords*.

Lord Justice Robert Lush, Kt

'A lawyer of all ages and systems with a career of unsurpassed utility.'

Chapter Three

Harvesting the Crop

As a judge, Robert was one of the most popular in his day even though he had never sought popularity and, 'whether on the Bench or in private life, was honoured by all who came in contact with him.' The next extract from the *Spectator* gives a lucid account of his judicial abilities:

'He had the art, which is possessed by so few of the judges, of cutting short irrelevant questions, giving the happy-despatch to bad points and trying a case with the utmost rapidity without offending anyone's feelings or perceptibly leaning to wither one side or the other. The truth is that, both intellectually and morally, he was peculiarly well equipped for the kind of work which he had to do. He was not only an accomplished lawyer but, what is much rarer, a lawyer who had perfect command over his resources and kept all his learning at his fingers' ends. His patience and thoroughness were so conspicuous and well-known that there was never the least reason to fear that a case tried by him would be 'scamped' or that the parties would be squeezed by judicial pressure into an unwilling compromise. He had, moreover, an unfailing urbanity which expressed itself in a demeanour full of dignified courtesy, not to say courtliness, and which was singularly attractive and winning in these days of relaxed etiquette. Sir Robert Lush, in short, preserved the best traditions of the English Bench. He was a strong judge without the least tincture of arrogance or self-assertion; a quick judge and yet, in the highest degree, cautious and painstaking; and a universally popular judge who never 'played to the gallery' or deviated by a hair's breadth from the line of strict impartiality.'

It is, therefore, hardly surprising that his abilities were also in demand elsewhere. When he wasn't in Court, he and his colleague, Sir George Jessel, were heavily involved with the framing of the rules under the *Judicature Act* of 1873, later amended in 1876, with the one representing the experience of the Common Law and the other that of Equity. (Broadly speaking, the *Judicature Act* was intended to simplify the tangle of legal institutions and procedures by bringing together several tribunals and creating a separate *Court of Appeal* and *High Court of Justice*.) And together with Justices Stephen and Barry and Lord Blackburn, Robert was also responsible for drafting the *Criminal Code* which was presented to Parliament in 1879 but never actually enacted.

However, despite Robert's steady progress up the judicial tree, the 1870's must have been a decade of mixed blessings. Certainly, there had been four marriages in his family: Mary's in 1871 to the Rev Hector McNeile, son of the Dean of Ripon; Caroline's in 1874 to a Yorkshire landowner and successful parliamentary barrister, Balfour Browne, who published a volume of reminiscences entitled *Forty Years at the Bar*; Herbert's in 1876 to Rose Wilson of Canon Pyon, Hereford; and Samuel's in 1878 to Harriet Susan of Erdeley Villa, Middlesborough. And, having gained a first class in the *Classical Tripos* at Cambridge, Montie was called to the Bar at *Gray's Inn* in 1879 only five months after Lord Beaconsfield had made his father a member of the *Privy Council*. But, on the 3rd April, 1870, his eldest son, Robert Christopher, died on the *SS Great Britain* en route for Australia; his sister-in-law, Harriet, who married his brother William, died of consumption only seven weeks later; and Samuel died at *Avenue Road* on the 21st July, 1878, only weeks after his marriage.

The distress caused by these deaths must have undoubtedly marred the joy of seeing another three of his children married but, true to form, Robert continued to perform his duties with the utmost vigour which must have been a great relief to both the courts and the public at large. The following two extracts provide an insight into the burdens of the judicial system at the time:

The Standard:

'...Indeed, there never yet was a time when English judges were more severely worked. In the old days a judge only sat during legal Term, while business at Assize was slight. Our great shipping ports and manufacturing industrial centres of activity had not then attained their present importance; and there was little, if any, business on

Assize of such serious importance as would in any way unduly swell the Motion List at Westminster Hall of appeals and motions for new trials. For the judge, indeed, the circuit was almost a holiday in itself, and he came back from it refreshed and invigorated, and not, as now, worn out with positive stress of labour and responsibility.'

The Times:

'Hilary Term opens today and the accustomed complaint rises of a superabundant harvest of litigation with few to reap it. A multitude of old causes stands over from last year with hundreds of new causes entered...The Spring Assizes are the dragon which thus decimates the judicial population because only a remnant of four judges of first instance is to be left within its precincts at most. The great majority will, by tonight, be as much dispersed as if the Chancellor's breakfast at the opening of Term were a breaking-up party before the holidays yet only a tithe of the issues which have been joined can, by reason of the judicial dearth, be determined. Nor is it to be supposed that the rest will solve themselves; they will stagnate, fester and poison. Were they all of a nature to be unravelled with ease and despatch, so vast a throng would still tax the utmost powers of an attenuated bench to marshall and dismiss. But among them are certain to be unwieldy and intricate monsters which will each devour without compunction the judicial time allotted for hundreds of expectant points of law or manageable questions of fact. Unless the same kind of exigency had been experienced often before, and had in some sort been survived, the extraordinary disproportion between the work to be done and the number of labourers to do it would produce a sense of blank despair.'

Likewise, Elizabeth was evidently as busy as ever with her work. Indeed, the extract below from one of the fathers on New Year's Day, 1878, gives the first indication, after the encounter with the reformed soldier, that she might have been pushing herself too hard for her own good:

'My Wish to our Dear Lady Lush

May the blessings of thy God wait upon thee and the sun of glory shine around thy head. May the gates of plenty, honour, and happiness be always open to thee and thine. May no strife disturb thy days nor sorrow disturb thy nights and may the pillow of peace kiss thy cheek and pleasures of imagination attend thy dreams. And when length of years makes thee tired of earthly joys and the curtains of death gently close round the scene of thy existence, may the angels of God attend thy bed. And take care that the expiring lamp of life shall not receive one rude blast to hasten its extinction. Finally, may the Saviour's blood wash thee from all impurities and, at last, usher thee into a land of everlasting felicity. God bless your dear husband, Sir Robert, and your sons and daughters. May the same blessings attend them. May they be like their dear mother, kind and tender hearted. Dear Lady, please accept this wish for a New Year's gift.

From one of your fathers.'

The second week of May, 1880, witnessed the commemoration of Dr Landels' 'Silver Wedding,' or twenty-five years of ministry, at *Regent's Park Chapel*. On the Sunday, the anniversary sermons were preached by Dr Landels before packed congregations with the minister giving details of the work of the church during the last quarter of a century. On the Tuesday afternoon, there was a service with a sermon preached by the Rev Spurgeon followed by a tea meeting held in the schoolroom and, subsequently, by a public meeting in the chapel, presided over by Sir Morton Peto, founder of the chapel. The platform was elaborately decorated and, besides Dr Landels, was occupied by Robert, Col Griffin, Samuel Chick, and the acting treasurer, Mr Benham. After the singing and prayers led by Mr Chick, the chairman gave an address 'in which he congratulated Dr Landels upon having been able to keep his health for twenty-five years and upon the work he had accomplished. He understood that £100,000 had been raised and used for the purposes of the church and that 2,000 members had passed through the Church during that period, there being now 600 members...' So the Church was in full swing, along with the *Mission Hall*, and Robert and Elizabeth were still actively involved with both. Elizabeth had now reached the age of sixty-two while her husband was in his seventy-third year but age was no impediment either to the progress of judges or to the work that needed to be done. It was quite common for the country's judges to be sitting in Court at the age of eighty – a tradition that still remains today, albeit to a lesser extent – and, by all accounts, it would appear that their judgements were not necessarily impaired by their advancing years. Some might even argue that they were enhanced! But, as far as Robert was concerned, rumours were beginning to circulate about him being tipped for the *Court of Appeal*. However, after fifteen years as a Puisne Judge, that immensely important period of Robert's life would not be complete without a description of his last case on Circuit:

'The last act of the new Lord Justice as a Puisne Judge has been to pronounce judgement in the Worcester election petition. He even found himself confronted with an objection on the part of the petitioners which they would never have raised had they not felt sure they were going to lose. They intimated to Mr Justice Lush that they did not consider him an election judge at all and got so far in whimsical Latinity as to pronounce him to be *defuncto officio*. He swept away the airy cobweb with a firm brush and he and Mr Justice Manisty proceeded to give their decision...Some judges are on Circuit while others are trying election petitions. The Lord Chief Justice has been indisposed and Baron Huddlestone has gone abroad for his health so the casual appearance of a judge at Westminster is greeted as a curious and pleasant chance, like the unexpected arrival of an old friend at Chamouni or Pontresina. Therefore, if, on any special occasion, we seem to be getting distinct good out of telling two judges to go to Worcester to hear what could be said about fifty-three alleged cases of bribery and fifteen cases of treating, such an occurrence deserves notice. As it happened, the judgement, which had to be pronounced at Worcester, was one which could not have been pronounced with equal effect by anyone but judges. The judgement consisted partly of a reprimand and partly of a nice adjudication on a point of mingled law and fact. The petitioners were severely and most justly censured for having got up a petition which they had scarcely anything to support and for making the gravest charges on the foundation of the most idle and malignant gossip. Their counsel had to abandon three-fourths of their cases of bribery and treating as utterly worthless and they had no evidence whatever to offer in support of the stinging charge of personal bribery which they had made against the sitting members...Such petitions deserve to be reprobated not only on moral grounds but as abuses of the machinery of justice. The only point raised by the petitioners which called for serious consideration had reference to the closing of two polling-booths before the hour of the close of the poll had struck. The judges seem to have felt so much doubt as to this that they twice had to put off the time when their judgement was pronounced. After due deliberation, they came to the conclusion that the polling-booths could not be said to have been technically closed before the appointed hour. Voting was interrupted, suspended or delayed but the returning officers never ceased to be willing and even anxious to do their duty. The legal meaning of the term 'closing' was, under the circumstances, so difficult to determine that it would have been unsatisfactory if the decision had been made by any but experienced and eminent lawyers.'

Nevertheless, even though it seemed almost certain that Robert would be elevated to the *Court of Appeal*, a certain degree of consternation was being, or had been, expressed as to why it had taken so long

by Lord Justice Thesiger himself, the man whom Robert succeeded:

'When the late Lord Justice Thesiger received his appointment, the name of Mr Justice Lush was on everybody's tongue and many of those best able to judge in such a matter felt that, but for political influences, the older and well-tried public servant (especially after the services he had rendered in connection with the Criminal Code) and not the younger man, who was then all but unknown to fame, would have been appointed to the office...If rumour is to be credited, Lord Justice Thesiger himself felt it a drawback to the satisfaction with which he received the appointment that he was coming in the way of another whose title to it was superior to his own.'

by the law press:

'The task of the Lord Chancellor becomes exceptionally hard when, as in the present case, one of the vacant posts is a place in the Court of Appeal. It is one of the few pieces of promotion for which the Judges are eligible as well as the members of the Bar. Those august persons not unnaturally dislike the sudden elevation of a man whom, until yesterday, they could snub with impunity into a position from which he can reverse their decisions, or, worse still, affirm the judgement of the Court below on different grounds. Mr Justice Lush has peculiarly strong claims. He is the senior Puisne Judge on the Bench and has twice been passed over when he might have fairly looked for promotion: once at the first formation of the Court of Appeal in favour of Sir Richard Amphlett and, again, on his retirement in favour of Mr Thesiger. His judgements, particularly on questions of commercial law are lucid and terse and are always treated with great respect. His appointment would give general satisfaction to the Bar and could excite no jealousy on the Bench.'

and by the press again:

'Whether in stuff or silk he was always a hard worker and it was probably on the well-known principle of working a willing horse that he was left to labour as an ordinary judge for fifteen years while many men neither abler nor more distinguished were promoted to less laborious offices. Perhaps some allowance must also be made for the fact that he never entered Parliament; and indeed, we believe, was not a thorough-going member of either political party. Theoretically, of course, politics and law ought not to have anything to do with one another. Practically, it will hardly be denied by anybody that they have.'

but not, apparently, by him:

After being congratulated by Mr Powell, QC, Mr Justice Lush replied: 'Mr Powell, and members of the Bar, I gratefully accept your kind expression of feeling. I hesitated a long time before I could make up my mind to give up a position I held on the Queen's Bench for fifteen years and to sever myself from honoured colleagues who made that position so comfortable and to whom I am under great obligation. After weighing all considerations, and especially the advice of my friends, I felt it a call of duty and obeyed it accordingly. I thank you for your kind and cordial expression.'

although the writer of this extract for the *Law Journal* expressed his concern because of the promotion:

'We had hoped to be able to record this week that the vacant judgeships had been completely filled up in readiness for the 2nd November but nothing has been done except, apparently, to move Mr Justice Lush from the Queen's Court to the Court of Appeal. The appointment of Mr Justice Lush as Lord Justice instead of Chief Baron, as had been hoped, makes us worse off than we were before. As a judge of first instance, Mr Justice Lush was equal to at least two average judges, to supply which gap we shall now have a judge with much to learn.'

and I can't resist this little analogy:

'Sir Robert Lush became a QC when Mr Thesiger was barely out of his teens and five years before he was called to the Bar. The careers of the two Judges when thus compared remind one of the fable of the hare and the tortoise: the younger man passed on swiftly to high dignity and honour but fell in the very midst of life while Sir Robert, born as long ago as 1807, is still with us and happily bears his now venerable years lightly. He may even yet not have reached the highest place which he is destined to obtain on the legal ladder.'

On the 5th November, 1880, Sir Robert Lush became a Lord Justice of Appeal whilst his son-in-law, Watkin Williams, filled his 'ordinary' seat on the *Queen's Bench*. And, to add to the general satisfaction of the legal profession and the public, there can be little doubt that his remaining family would have been as delighted as the Baptists, especially since he was the first Baptist to have 'ever held such exalted office in England.' However, Tragedy was on the march once again. By this time, Elizabeth was already gravely ill and, for the past nine months, had been suffering from consumption, the same illness that had cost her younger sister, Harriet, her life. Despite the fact that she had now been ill for some time, she had tried hard to conceal its true nature from her family for fear of distressing them and, against the advice of her doctor, Dr Wilbe of

Finchley Road, continued to carry out her duties both at the *Mission Hall* and at the Church to the best of her ability. On Christmas Eve of that year, when as many as six hundred poor people from the neighbourhood had been invited for the customary Christmas dinner at *Regent's Park Chapel*, she insisted on standing at the door to wish each one of their guests a happy Christmas. Despite being urged not to over exert herself, she had insisted on being there, saying, 'But what if it should be the last opportunity I have of speaking to them?' And she stood at that door until her illness forced her to retire to bed. She almost had to be carried to her carriage.

As it happened, that was indeed the last occasion on which she appeared in public. Shortly before five o'clock on the morning of Wednesday, the 16th March, 1881, she called her loved ones to her bedside, knowing that she had little time left. She bade them farewell and conveyed a final message to the Church and to all those whom she cared for: 'Give my love to the Church,' she said, 'and to my poor people, and tell them I did love them so.' To her youngest daughter, Florence, she also added that she was leaving her in charge of the *Mission Hall*, a prospect which the latter didn't greatly relish owing to her frail disposition but a trust which, as we shall see in due course, she honoured most admirably. And perhaps we can guess what Elizabeth might have said to her dear husband after forty-two years of friendship, love and all the joys that their marriage would have encompassed.

It had been suggested that a funeral service at the Chapel might precede her removal to the family vault at Kensal Green cemetery but, due to the strain that would have imposed on the family, it was decided to settle for a short service at *Avenue Road*. There were over a thousand mourners at the funeral on this bitterly cold Monday afternoon, a figure totally unprecedented in the history of London for what was known as an 'ordinary funeral.' And the following extracts from *The Baptist* and *The Indicator* reveal that, in modern parlance, it was anything but ordinary for these were no ordinary people:

'A procession of four mourning coaches and twenty private carriages with numerous conveyances containing the old mothers and the aged and infirm of the Drummond Street Mission as well as a long line of pedestrians from Marylebone and Kentish Town followed the hearse from the house of Lord Justice Lush to the place of interment. In the road in front of the residence for some time before the cortege moved off, a large number of spectators were assembled whose looks testified both to their regard for the departed and their sympathy with the bereaved family; for, to a wide circle in the neighbourhood, her good deeds were well known. Along the line of the route to the cemetery also it seemed as if many of the residents had obtained knowledge of whose funeral it was that was passing, as well as of her previous life, because, here and there from their windows or groups in the road, they looked on with a respectful, sympathetic interest such as we have never observed at any ordinary funeral. Boys from the neighbourhood of the Mission Hall accompanied the procession on foot the whole of the way and, on nearing the cemetery, working men and their wives from the same neighbourhood and mothers with children by their side and infants in their arms were seen wending their way thither, eager to be there in time for the funeral obsequies. The numbers that had gathered round the grave extended some distance outside the gate and along a lane formed by the crowd, which divided itself into two, the coffin, covered with flowers and followed by the mourners, was slowly drawn amidst the tears and sobs of those who stood on either side. Very few public men, how ever much admired, were ever honoured with such marks of affection from the lowly as was shown that day by the hundreds of poor mothers who wept over the grave. But the greater number were poor people to whom the loss of a day meant considerable diminution of their already too scanty resources. Others knew what a loving, amiable, generous and valuable co-worker they had lost. It was not cold admiration for public acts which brought them there but affection as for a sister and gratitude to a benefactor and friend. And now that they were to see her face, hear her voice, feel the warm clasp of her hand and receive her friendly greeting no more, no wonder that their tears and sobs could not be repressed.'

In the words of the *Christian Age*, 'Few of the large-hearted, philanthropic, Christian ladies of the Metropolis will be more missed than the estimable wife of Lord Justice Lush,' and, needless to say, the tributes right across the press, even as far as Philadelphia, were numerous. However, being the sort of person she was, Elizabeth would not thank me for oversinging her praises so I will restrict myself to just two extracts, the first from the funeral sermon of Dr Landels and, perhaps even more fittingly, the second from one of her mothers:

'Whoever else might be absent from their post, she was always to be found at hers. If her place was not filled at any time, everyone knew that it was either illness or absence from town which was the cause. No invitation to party, concert or entertainment of any kind was accepted nor any engagement formed which prevented her attendance at the weekly meeting. No one surpassed her in courtesy to her friends but no call or visit of friend was ever allowed to keep her away from the house of God. She could have enjoyed occasional changes such as social gatherings and visits to places of recreation but the church arrangements to which she had consented were deemed as binding as a solemn contract and no external inducement could lead her to violate her pledge. The workers in the church sought her counsel and the poor in their troubles sought her sympathy and help and in neither case did they have to seek in vain. Most of us know something of the interest she took in her mothers. How happy she was to see them assemble in crowds at the annual tea-meeting to which she invited them here and, still more, at the annual summer gathering in the grounds adjoining her residence.

Not knowing for a time the serious nature of her illness, I was not quite satisfied with the treatment she was undergoing and would sometimes express my conviction that a change might be beneficial. And never can I forget the quiet smile with which she would receive my statement, a smile which I can now too well understand and which even then seemed to say, 'Ah, but you do not know how grave my ailment is.' Sometimes, she did say in words, 'Wait until this plan has had a fair trial and then I will go to any medical man you may desire.' I had begun, indeed, to suspect what the illness was before the full sad revelation came but it was difficult to admit the suspicion that it could be anything so fearful when she appeared so composed. After the Chapel Dinner on Christmas Eve, she never left her home and was only once able to join the family circle so that her life may be said to have fitly closed with a grand exercise of the self-denial by which it had been so much distinguished. She had much reason for wishing to live. Her husband had received the well-deserved honours which crowned his judicial course and she was not incapable of appreciating them. And no mother was ever more beloved. Numerous grandchildren, too, were growing up around her in whom the love of her own children was reproduced. She had a wide circle of friends, among whom she was a general favourite and, as Treasurer of the Zenana Mission, she had seen the society grow from its comparatively small beginning to its present dimensions. Moreover, the mothers, of whom she had four or five hundred in her class, regarded her with the profoundest gratitude and reverence.

On confinement to her chamber, she would often quote Bunyan (famous for 'imprinting some of the characteristic religious attitudes of the Dissenters indelibly on the English consciousness'): 'More pilgrims are come to town...And so many went over the water and were let in at the golden gates today...Then the pilgrims got up and walked to and fro but how their ears now filled with heavenly voices and their eyes delighted with celestial visions!' She said to me once, 'Is it not strange that I have had such a happy life and feel so happy now?' At first, I did not quite understand her but, afterwards, saw her meaning to be that, after having had such a happy life, it was strange she should feel so happy at the thought of leaving it. Strange it was in one sense but not in another: strange that the thought of leaving so much happiness should awaken no regret but not strange in view of the higher joy beyond.

A mortal dies and an immortal is born. Earth becomes poorer that heaven may be enriched and the soul is freed from its earthly trammels that it may enter on the state and condition of an angel of God. Notwithstanding our loss, we are richer today because she has been with us and the fragrance of her life will abide with us long after she is gone. Memories like hers are fraught with holy influences and, from graves like hers, some better purpose springs. May it be so in our experience!

Finally, let us pray that he, who has lost his dear partner in life, may have God's smile resting on his now comparatively lonely way and that his sons and daughters may be faithful to their mother's memory and distinguished by their mother's virtues.'

And from the mother:

We loved her, how we loved her,
But her Saviour loved her more
And now she is safely resting
On Canaan's peaceful shore.

Oh happy saint!
May we, like thee, be blest;
In life, like thee, be faithful;
Like thee, in death, find rest.

M.A.R.

March 16th,1881

****

1880-81 was not only a traumatic time for the Lush family but for many other people as well. On the 18th January, London was almost cut off by a savage snowstorm, an earthquake at Scio buried 5,000 people and left another 4,000 homeless, Benjamin Disraeli died and there was a cholera epidemic at Mecca. The *Opera House* at Nice and the *Ring Theatre* at Vienna were both burnt to the ground, there was an explosion at the Wigan colliery and a fatal accident on the Canonbury railway. Mass panic in a Warsaw Church resulted in a number of deaths, storms in London on the 14th October destroyed most of its trees and, to cap it all, Mr Powell had lost his balloon!

However, shortly after Elizabeth's death in March, Robert's health also went into serious decline. Despite the comfort he will have received from his family, colleagues and members of the Church, there can be little doubt that the loss of his beloved wife had already taken its toll on him. It was hoped, by many, that he might be able to recuperate during the Long Vacation and, certainly, he managed to make something of a comeback for the *Court of Appeal* that autumn. On the 3rd December, Robert heard the case of *Shardlow v Cotterell* with the Master of the Rolls, George Jessel, and Lord Justice Bagallay. The issue was one of contractual definition relating to the

Statute of Frauds and was questioning the vagueness of the word 'property.' Did property refer to real estate or goods and chattels? But as Robert points out in his judgement, the contract in this case clearly states that, since the expenses of the transfer of the property are to be paid by the purchaser, it should be sufficiently clear that the property in question was the building being sold, other items not being passed by conveyance: 'There is no transfer if you buy a horse or anything of that kind.' He then goes on to explain why he thought that the previous judge, Mr Justice Kay, had raised the issue of uncertainty in the first place and concludes that, in his enthusiasm, his learned brother had overlooked the conditions of sale which, to his mind, showed quite clearly 'that the property was real estate.' Mr Shardlow, therefore, was presumably entitled to the building he had just purchased and not just the cutlery.

And with that case behind bars, Robert was expected to sit again in *Lincoln's Inn* on the 12th December but his health quickly deteriorated to such an extent that he was unable to make another court appearance. Dr Landels describes his closing days with characteristic compassion:

'In his latter days he seemed to us to show a wonderful ripening for the final change. The death of his wife, with whom he had lived in such loving fellowship for so many years, was a terrible trial to him and, though he strove bravely to bear up under it, the shock it gave to his gentle nature was one from which he never quite recovered. She told him before her departure that he would not be long in following and, to those of us who noticed his failing strength, it soon appeared that her words would prove true. He gradually sank and, with the gradual sinking of the physical frame, there was a gradual development of all the finer qualities of his nature...A peculiar gentleness characterised his closing days, a mellowing of character as if ripening for a better world and, when the end came, he was like a shock of corn fully ripe. Gently, he passed away like a wearied child falling asleep, mercifully suffering little. The last words of the great judge were: 'Not my will but Thine be done.'

It was on Monday, the 27th December, 1881, at about 10am that the great judge passed away, the fifth to have vacated the *Court of*

Appeal involuntarily in little more than a year, and, just as there had been a private ceremony at *Avenue Road* prior to the funeral procession of his wife, there was another prior to his own on the 2nd January, 1882. These amalgamated accounts from the press describe the sequel in some detail:

'One o'clock was the hour appointed for the interment but the funeral cortege, which made its way from Regent's Park via Queen's Road and Marlborough Road, did not reach the cemetery until a considerable time after the appointed hour. It consisted of an ordinary hearse carrying the coffin and drawn by a pair of horses followed by the family carriage and seven mourning coaches. A large number of private carriages joined in the mournful procession, amongst them being those of the Lord Mayor and Lady Lycett and most of the officials of the Superior Courts whilst Messrs Richard and Wright attended as part of a deputation from the Deputies of the Protestant Dissenters which included the Evangelical Alliance, the Baptist Union and the London Baptist Association. The long string of carriages stretched up the road for some distance and formed part of the procession on the way to the cemetery. A vast concourse, composed of nearly all classes, there awaited the approach of the hearse and, on its arrival, formed themselves into an avenue through which the coffin, whose outer oak case contained a lead coffin and an elm shell, was slowly drawn to the grave on wheels. The uncovered heads, as it approached, were a genuine token of the respect in which the deceased was held and the tears in many eyes spoke of the still warmer feelings with which they followed him to his tomb. The Elders of the church in Regent's Park, of which, as our readers know, the deceased had been an officebearer for ten years, walked on each side of the coffin from the gate to the cemetery and many of the poor from the neighbourhood of the Mission Hall were there, as on the occasion of Lady Lush's funeral, to testify their regard for the benefactor they had lost. But, perhaps the most touching testimony to the memory of the deceased was the presence of twelve boys and twelve girls from the Orphan Working School at Haverstock Hill, which was generously supported by the late Judge, who presided at their last annual meeting, and by Lady Lush who was chairwoman of the Ladies' Committee of that institution.

Although the year was not eight-and-forty hours old, the famous *Pere la Chaise* of London had already received a batch of new tenants and there were two other funerals proceeding in other parts of the burial ground but, for some time previously, groups of persons had surrounded the family vault and lingered long over the sight of the darkening coffins exposed to view. The flowers and wreaths, and the baskets that contained them, were decayed into a uniform dolorous brown upon the coffin of Lady Lush though all the tokens of affection, even to the leaves and sprays, retained their shape. Below there lay the remains of other members of the family: the eldest son, Robert Christopher, the third son, Samuel Clarence, Lady Lush's mother, Elizabeth Ann Woollacott, and a baby of 14 months, Lucy Elizabeth, whose little black coffin was lowest of all. The brightly-polished oak and brass mountings enclosing the late head of the family in due time eclipsed these tarnished relics but, so long as they remained exposed, they seemed to offer an irresistible fascination to the living who clustered round. A number of wreaths were sent by personal friends and others, amongst them being a beautiful specimen from the Leeds Branch of the Anglo-Jewish Association and another from the Avenue Road domestics 'as a respectful tribute to the memory of their much beloved master' and many members of the Baptist Chapel in Regent's Park were also present.

The committal sentences of the service were read by the Rev Dr Landels and the coffin-lid was covered with garlands of flowers, completely hiding the inscription which simply stated that the Right Honourable Robert Lush, Lord Justice of Appeal, was born on the 25th Oct, 1807 and died on the 27th Dec, 1881.'

And, just as there had been a torrent of tributes to Elizabeth, there was another for Robert from which I have selected the following cross-section:

The Standard:

'Lord Justice Lush was by the common consent not of the profession only, but of the general public, one of the most learned amongst Her Majesty's Judges. Although no orator, he was a consummate lawyer and, above all, was known to be of unblemished honour, incapable of misrepresentation or exaggeration. In that particular class of Nisi Prius cases which is chiefly watched for by the general public he was not largely concerned. But he soon acquired a heavy mercantile practice and his opinion on doubtful points of law was in universal request. His career has been uneventful but not on that account the less dignified. He was never a politician and never sat in the House of Commons, nor was he ever one of the Law Officers of the Crown but he had the most unbounded confidence of the profession, of litigants and of the public. He was a most painstaking and conscientious judge. He made it his duty, in every case that came before him, to search into the merits and to seek out every point, either of law or of fact, how ever minute. He thus acquired a reputation for that vast impartiality which, in reality, he possessed. But it was further known that he would be a thoroughly impartial judge, incapable of going beyond the facts on the record or of allowing any extraneous circumstances, how ever notorious, to influence his decision. His elevation to the Court of Appeal was also a matter of certainty and the only wonder in connection with it was that it should have been so long delayed for, in truth, the powers of Sir Robert Lush were wasted at Nisi Prius and his full strength and immense impartiality only came out when a vexed point of law had to be argued.'

source unknown:

'Lord Justice Lush was a judge whom it will be very difficult to replace. He was not, perhaps, distinctly a brilliant man nor was his intellect, though fine, in any way extraordinary. But he had that well-balanced mind and temperament which are rarer, and often more useful, than the possession of some conspicuous intellectual gift. Brilliant men have failed in every walk of life: Lord Justice Lush would have succeeded in any. He combined common sense and common law in a remarkable way. He enjoyed in a high degree the confidence of the profession while his conspicuous fairness, unfailing courtesy and dignity made him a judge of great authority with suitors and the public. He saw the birth of the new judicial system and no man was better able to carry it out in the spirit as well as in the letter. He was engaged also with Sir James Stephen in drawing and revising the Criminal Code Bill which will become law some time this century. We cannot shut our eyes to the fact that neither the Bench nor the Bar have any special reason to look back with satisfaction to that nightmare of the Tichborne trial but, assuredly, Sir Robert might have done so with more equanimity than his associates.'

source unknown:

'If the late Lord Justice Lush could have cherished one regret, it must have been that his upward rise was not so continuous as his first successes seemed to guarantee...His legal acumen was penetrating and his style of address perspicacious. Not only was he a sound lawyer but he was a man of the world with the sympathies and sense which a man of the world has acquired. He was always ready with almost paternal advice to suitors and, if he could persuade them to compromise the case out of Court, he was well pleased. To discover what was best for both parties was his guiding motive and, when the heat of the litigation had cooled down, all were willing to acknowledge his services as a mediator. Then, his good nature was great and young counsel had often to be grateful for a kind word in their perplexities.

There are few judges whose careers have spanned an epoch of change with such success. Recent legislation has turned our system of law from the most technical into one of the most untechnical in the world but Lord Justice Lush, whose fame in the first instance was founded on technicalities, ever kept pace with change and proved himself a lawyer of all ages and systems. He did not let the mutability of things get the better of him and has left behind him the name of a sound judge. That is a sufficient title to praise without reckoning in those qualities of temper and character which make men look on the dead with affection as well as with respect.'

Truth:

'Few English Judges have done more towards the simplification of our law than Lord Justice Lush. The one great and prominent fact in his judicial life, which contrasted him so strongly with his brother

Justices, was his keen insight into the moral as well as the legal merits of such claims as came before him, relying upon which he was enabled to decided cases on their own merits instead of being tied down by those hard and fast rules of precedent which obtain so widely in the profession.'

source unknown:

'It has been said that a great general is usually rather anxious to avoid battle than to engage in it and, in somewhat the same way, it was a characteristic of Lord Justice Lush, as a judge, to prevent suitors if he could from litigating. Nor was he wont to 'bait' counsel who might not distinguish themselves by an extraordinary display of knowledge or intelligence in their arguments. In short, few of his fellows have left the Bench with a better record, as well intellectually as morally, as well morally as from the point of view of business aptitudes and professional skill.'

Sir George Jessel, Master of the Rolls:

'As a member of the Committee of Judges, which revised and settled the rules under the Judicature Act, he gave willing and most efficient assistance. Those who knew him in private life, knew him as kind and benevolent, pleasant in manner and amiable in disposition. As a judge we can truly say that he was conscientious, painstaking, patient and impartial, administering the law with sound learning and sound sense.'

Charles Reade:

'*Non omnis mortuus est.* The departed judge still teaches from his tomb; his *dicta* will outlive him in our English courts; his *gesta* are for mankind.'

The losses of Robert and Elizabeth Lush will have therefore been felt by many in the legal profession, the Church at Regent's Park, the *Mission Hall* and all the charities with which they were involved. There must have been literally hundreds of people who would have been either directly or indirectly affected by their departure but, fortunately, through the practice of the revised English legal system, which has only recently been modified, the current concern that our missionaries show for third world countries, and the continued service to the church of Hampstead by current members of the family, their extraordinary legacy lives on.

Non omnis mortuus est

The Rt Hon Sir Charles Montague Lush, Kt
Chapter Four

New Beginnings

Perhaps the most notable difference between Sir Robert and Sir Charles Montague Lush was their preparation for adult life; whereas Robert had been taught at the local school and continued to learn what he could by way of practical experience at Mr Chitty's office, 'Montie' approached the Bar with a superior education, and his father's relative wealth, behind him. In September, 1866, he began his school career at *Westminster School*, the oldest school in London to have remained on its original site since 1179 and whose old boys have included names like Ben Jonson, Christopher Wren, Sir Adrian Boult and Sir John Gielgud. And in the summer of 1872, he left with a Triplett before entering *Trinity Hall*, Cambridge where he matriculated in the Michaelmas term of that year, was a scholar from 1873-76 and gained a 1st class in the *Classical Tripos*. There can be little doubt that he was a most diligent student and one of his university notebooks contains extracts from the *Gospel according to St Luke* in Greek and Milton's *Paradise Lost* in Latin, all written in a meticulous hand; certainly, the only indication of a wandering mind can be found in his scenic sketches at the top of those pages relating to Aristotle's politics but this came as no surprise to me since his father had shown so little interest in the affairs of government. Then, having been admitted to *Gray's Inn* on the 19th October, 1874, Montie began his studies as a Law student in 1876 and was called to the Bar on the 7th May, 1879 without having to use a wife's dowry to pay his fees!

However, once he had been called to the Bar, the next stage of his career must have followed a close parallel with that of his father. As we know, Robert had secured a promising post at Mr Bishop's office when he first went to London and Montie was fortunate enough to have secured a place in the chambers of Mr Henn Collins, who was destined to become one of the great judges of the day, occupying the positions of Puisne Judge, Lord Justice of Appeal and Master of the Rolls all within the space of twenty years. Moreover, if Robert had acquired clients through the Nonconformist network, his son undoubtedly acquired some of his through the reputation of his father and, as juniors, both father and son were extremely busy, popular and successful. All the same, Robert had had no one to emulate whereas Montie had and his father's reputation must have been a hard act to follow. Indeed, his elder brother, Herbert, who was a member of the *Inner Temple*, decided not to even try, perhaps wisely settling for a County Court Judgeship and a brief fling in the political arena – he was Conservative candidate for East Northants in 1895 but lost to the Liberals who had already held the seat for ten years. Nevertheless, not only was Montie a brave man who fought hard for the underdog but I have little doubt that his ambition to equal, if not surpass, the reputation of his father was fired largely by an absolute reverence for his father and, perhaps, a grateful appreciation of the early educational advantages which Robert had been denied. He had a duty to succeed and, all things being equal, which they never are, nothing was going to stand in his way.

'Courageous to a fault', as one columnist described him, Montie soon found himself in great demand as a junior barrister. Small in stature, just like his father, 'his gentle tones seemed to disqualify him for jury practice but, to the surprise of his friends, he developed unsuspected gifts of advocacy.' And as Lord Birkenhead said: 'His lachrymatory eloquence, combined with appearance of complete simplicity and candour often secured unexpected verdicts.' However, Montie was not the only son of a judge to be ploughing his furrow and many of his peers, who were also to become judges, were enhancing their professional status by writing books, a practice which, by now, had almost become mandatory; Vaughan Williams had written a book on bankruptcy law, Farwell on powers, Buckley on company law and Phillimore on ecclesiastical and international law. So in the wake of the *Married Woman's Property Act* of 1882, Montie's first publication *The Law of Husband and Wife* was published two years later, echoing his father's literary achievements and, likewise, becoming the standard book on the subject for many years. I don't suppose he was too dissatisfied with the following review but he may have wondered whether he had chosen the right title:

'The Law of Husband and Wife forms a most important branch of Jurisprudence and has an interest of its own apart from the mere legal aspect of the various questions involved. It deals not only with what may be called purely personal law but also embraces much of the law of Property. The recent changes of the law tend more and more to regard husband and wife not in any peculiar proprietary relation towards one another but to render them as competent as actual strangers to enter into mutual transactions affecting their property. Mr Lush has lately given to the profession a work on this subject. It is the first distinct treatise of its kind since Mr MacQueen's work and covers a far wider field than the recent textbooks on the Married Woman's Property Act. And yet, we are of the opinion that the learned author has been hampered in his design by that piece of legislation and has been at more pains to trace out the visible and potential changes wrought in the law by the Act than to set out in comprehensive form a general view of the law within the scope of his design. It is true that he limits his labours to the law within the jurisdiction of the Queen's Bench and Chancery Divisions but a good deal of law connected with husband and wife lies outside of that jurisdiction. We are not quite sure but that the more accurate title of the work would be, 'A Criticism of the Law of Husband and Wife.' There is scarcely a dictum of decision, germane to the matter in hand, which is not uncompromisingly laid bare by the scalpel of the author; sometimes it survives the operation while, at others, it succumbs and is ruthlessly put on one side. Mr Lush has the courage of his opinions; his criticisms are not merely ingenious but are characterised by a thorough knowledge of the law and he not infrequently adduces strong reasons to support his conclusions. The effect of this treatment is to make the book admirable reading but to leave the reader less with an idea of what the law is than of what Mr Lush thinks it ought to be. Though the work is uneven, it evinces throughout much care and thought. The chapter on Separation Deeds is, in our opinion, the best in the book and is an admirable specimen of treatise writing; again, the one on the Contracts of married women is very good; but the one dealing with Marriage Settlements is only indifferently good and the first chapter, that on the general incidents of the marriage relation, is thin and discursive. Mr Lush has one thing to recommend him most strongly and that is his accuracy; therefore his book is one which everyone may consult with the assurance that all the leading recent authorities are quoted and that the statements of law are supported by actual decisions. A little pruning and condensing would improve the value of the book but, on the whole, the learned author deserves well of the profession for the considerable pains he has taken in dealing with his subject and the excellent style in which it is presented to the public.'

And, in 1887, the year of Queen Victoria's first Jubilee, Montie published another, perhaps less remarkable, book entitled *Married Women's Rights and Liabilities* which mainly concerned itself with issues such as liabilities, assurance, civil and criminal proceedings, and breaches of trust.

Mr Montague Lush, KC: 'courageous to a fault.'

****

However, before we get too involved with Montie's work at the Bar, this would seem to be an opportune moment to take a look at what was happening in the lives of his siblings since sixteen years had now passed since the deaths of Robert and Elizabeth. You may recall that, at that time, Florence, was the only unmarried daughter and that it was to her that Elizabeth had left the running of the *Mission Hall* and flats with the words, 'God will give you all you need to carry on the work.' Until then, Florence had not been able to play an active part at the hall on account of her health although she was well-acquainted with all the work behind the scenes. And, indeed, help was at hand. Firstly, Dr Angus' eldest daughter, Edith, took on the leadership of the Wednesday meeting with Florence to help her while the latter had the oversight of all the premises and the responsibility of the tenants, all of whom she knew personally. And secondly, Montie took charge of the *Men's Bible Class*, playing an important role in the Mission's activities for the rest of his life. However, the greatest possible assistance must have come from Alfred Pearce Gould who was more than ready to share in all her responsibilities and activities and whom Florence married in 1885. (His first wife, Katherine Heelas of Wokingham, and a member of the family who owned the *Heelas* department store in Reading, had died in 1882.) Together, they built the *Men's Club Room* in memory of Robert and Elizabeth and he must have been very familiar with all the work carried out under the umbrella of the *Domestic Mission* which continued to thrive. Its first missionary from the *London City Mission*, Mr Thomas, was succeeded by Mr Brown and Mr Sutterby and Dorothy Pearce Gould describes some of the wonderful work carried out by the Mission at the turn of the century:

'Those were days of heart-rending poverty, terrible drunkenness and street fights; many a time was Mr Sutterby called in to intervene and many were the lives he led out of darkness into light. Under his leadership, the work thrived: the Penny Bank was the largest in London; a Men's Slate Club did a fine work; the Christmas Goose Club was more than a rival for that run by the public house, hundreds of geese being distributed on Christmas Eve. Temperance work held a large place both among adults and in the Band of Hope and the Men's Club and Bible Class flourished. Lodging houses were visited and there was an annual supper for 'down-and-outs.' In this special work, great help was given by the Mission Band, started by Mr Meyer at Regent's Park College in 1890, and, every Sunday evening, after the evening service, the Mission Band went into the open air and lodging houses. Many were the young men who received their first training in Christian work and not a few enlisted later in the Baptist Missionary Society or kindred societies. And many a Baptist Minister today recalls being sent to preach at the Mission Hall while a student at the College.'

She also describes how the *Baptist Sisterhood* was founded in 1898 and how the Mission was served with great devotion by the Angus sisters and a long succession of Deaconesses despite the unprecedented effects of two World Wars. And after a heartfelt plea for further support to reach the 'multitudes of men and women outside the fold,' Dorothy concludes with a quotation from Malachi which her grandmother, Elizabeth, would have surely deemed most fitting: 'And they shall be mine, saith the Lord of Hosts, in that day when I make up my jewels.'

Florence's husband, the 'kindly surgeon', Alfred Pearce Gould, was born in Norwich in 1852, the second son of the Rev George Gould, an eminent Baptist Minister. He was educated at *Amersham Hall* and the *University College of London Medical School*, graduating at *London University* in 1874. He was created a KCVO (Knight Commander of the Victorian Order) in 1911 and awarded a CBE in 1919 for recognition of his work during the war when he was in charge of the Surgical Division of the *Third London Military Hospital* at Wandsworth and the following list of titles will give some indication of the high esteem in which he was held: Vice Chancellor of the *University of London*; President of the *Boys' Life Brigade*; President of the Clinical Section of the *Royal Society of Medicine*; President of the *Medical Society of London*; Master in Surgery at *London University*; Fellow of the *Royal Society of Surgeons of England*; Consultant Surgeon, Emeritus Lecturer and Dean at the *Middlesex Hospital*; President of the *Rontgen Society*; Treasurer of the *Regent's Park Chapel*. He was also responsible for several publications on Medicine, one of the most notable being *The*

Elements of Surgical Analysis.

As well as being highly respected, Alfred was obviously a very busy man and one may wonder how he found the time to assist Florence at the *Mission Hall*. One may also wonder how Florence found the time to raise five children, who either grew up to lead distinguished lives themselves or produced another generation that did, and indulge her passion for salmon fishing at Dulverton on the Exe and at Holne Chase on the Dart. Apparently, she was a very skilful fisherman and her greenheart salmon rod, not the lightest of instruments compared to today's carbon fibre rods, still presides over one of the family walls in the west country. Their eldest daughter, Florence Eileen, married Charles Thomas Le Quesne in 1916, an accomplished barrister who worked in the chambers of one of Montie's greatest rivals, Sir Edward Carson after the First World War and was heavily tipped to become a judge of the High Court. Unfortunately, this never materialised although he did become a KC in 1925 and was twice appointed Commissioner of Assize. Being a profoundly religious man and President of the *Baptist Union* of Great Britain and Ireland in 1946, he will long be remembered for his outstanding service to the people of Jersey, having played a major role in helping the Channel Islands Refugees during the Second World War. Florence and Alfred's eldest son, Leslie, showed great promise as a surgeon but his life was tragically cut short, like so many, during the last year of the Great War in France. And their child, Eric, who had been a science scholar at *Christchurch*, Oxford, held the rank of Rear Admiral as a temporary surgeon during that war and, like his father, became Dean of the *Middlesex Hospital* as well as President of the *Medical Defence Union*. Their other two daughters, Hilda Dorothy and Evelyn Marjorie never married but were known to have provided great assistance at the *Mission Hall*. And as for their grandchildren, Thomas and Eileen's eldest son, Charles Martin, entered the Foreign Service, became successively Ambassador in Mali and Algeria, High Commissioner in Nigeria and served in the States of Jersey as Deputy for Saint Saviour from 1978-1990; he was created a KCMG in 1974. Leslie Philip became Professor of Surgery at the *Middlesex Hospital Medical School* in 1963 and Dean of the Faculty of Medicine at *London University* in 1980; he was awarded a CBE in 1984. Godfray became Chairman of the Council of *Regent's Park College* in 1958, Chairman of the *Monopolies and Mergers Commission* in 1975 and Treasurer of the *Inner Temple* in 1989; he has also been an Appeal Judge for Jersey and Guernsey and was knighted at Buckingham Palace in 1980. And the youngest member of this family, Susan, was a missionary in East Pakistan and Bangladesh for many years as well as Chairman of the *Baptist Mission Society* in 1991-1992. Quite some record of achievement in three generations of one family!

Had Florence's younger brother, Percy John Frederick, my great-grandfather, not lost his life in 1918, he might have also gained honours for his work in the medical missionary field but, nevertheless, the contribution he did make is certainly worthy of attention. (Exactly why Herbert was the least favoured in Robert's Will while Percy and Florence tipped the scales the other way is not clear. Possibly, this was simply because the latter were the youngest children with the least security or perhaps it had something to do with their strong, religious convictions which their parents hoped would bear fruit and which did. Nonetheless, it is interesting to note that, rather than apportioning his estate in equal measures to each of his surviving children, with allowances for the two widows, he made the distribution according to a sliding scale.) After his career at *Westminster School*, Percy was elected to *Christchurch* in 1876 where he matriculated on the 13th October of that year. He then gained a BA in 1880, an MA in 1884 and an MRCS in 1887 before establishing a medical practice in South Hampstead where he obviously tried to cure his patients with the Gospel as well as the more standard prescriptions. At that time, there was a weekly visitation of a *Medical Mission* with which he was involved in *Gough Street, Gray's Inn Road*, organised by the *Baptist Deaconesses' Home and Mission*. Percy soon became known as 'The Penny Doctor' because, although treatment was free, a collection was taken at the short service which was an integral part of each Friday afternoon clinic with Percy and the Deaconesses in training taking it in turns to give the address. Sympathetic to the idea of a *Medical Mission Auxiliary*, it was Percy who arranged the opening informal discussions with representatives of the *Baptist Mission Society* and the circle was then widened by the inclusion of Alfred Pearce Gould 'partly because of the family connection but still more on account of his eminence as a Christian surgeon.' This little group of doctors then brought the issue of the *Medical Auxiliary* before the officers of the *Baptist Mission Society* not only with the aim of maintaining all the existing medical agencies of the BMS and *Baptist Zenana Mission* but also with the intention of multiplying them by sending out additional qualified medical missionaries. Their recommendation was approved, a constitution was drafted and Percy was appointed Chairman of the new *Medical Mission Auxiliary* in 1901, a position which he held for the rest of his life. Indeed, such was his enthusiasm for this project, the *Medical Fund* flourished, increasing from £458 in 1903 to £24,000 in 1925. One of the smaller funds under its umbrella was the *Medical Aid Fund* which enabled grants to be made to Baptist medical students needing financial aid during their training and, akin to this, was the Scholarship Fund, launched in 1919 as a memorial to Percy and also designed to assist in medical training.

After a stint as a medical missionary himself during the late 1880's at Dorrington in Sierra Leone, Percy married Lydia Anderson, the second daughter of W.D.Anderson of Frognal, Hampstead in July, 1891, and they had two children, Ronald William and Joan, both of whom became doctors. Joan was one of the nation's first women doctors and practised at Southend. She never married but was warmly remembered by her two nephews, Warren and Robin, who also followed the family medical tradition, as a benevolent aunt who kept a much-beloved Highland Terrier. Interestingly, Ronald worked as a clerk for his uncle, Montie, before he qualified as a GP and settled in Midhurst, W.Sussex, where he married the daughter of Joseph Warren Smallwood, Chairman of a long-established wines and spirits business, and Kathleen Rashleigh Herrick, a descendant of the family of 17th century poet, Robert Herrick. However, unlike his other uncle, Watkin Williams, Ronald couldn't be persuaded to exchange his white coat for a wig and gown. Nor could his wife's ancestry encourage him to take up the pen.

****

In 1893, Montie was raised to the Bench of *Gray's Inn* and the following extract from the *Morning Leader* describes how he began to enhance a reputation already heralded by his skills as an author and his 'unsuspected gifts of advocacy':

'Mr Montague Lush has certainly had a most remarkable career but, a few years ago, his name was unknown, excepting that it belonged to the son – a young man of a rather dilettante disposition – of the late Lord Justice. A few years later a learned work revealing considerable research and wide knowledge appeared from his pen on The Law of Husband and Wife. This work attracted attention and then it was recalled that its author was the young man who devilled so well for Mr Archibalds, a gentleman who is now one of the Masters in Chancery. When Mr Archibalds was appointed to the Mastership, Mr Lush had his opportunity which he seized. The result is that he now has all the enormous practice which Mr Archibalds held and that there is probably no more successful junior at the Bar.'

Indeed, with such a successful practice, many of his colleagues were beginning to wonder why he hadn't applied for silk but, apparently, he was too busy to even contemplate such a thing!

Fortunately, however, he was not too busy to find himself a wife. We shall probably never know exactly how he met Margaret Abbie Locock although her mother, Fanny, must surely have been acquainted with Elizabeth through the *Zenana Mission* since they were both active office-bearing participants: Elizabeth had been Treasurer while Fanny had been a Vice-President and Honorary Secretary of the Paddington Branch until her death in August, 1889. Furthermore, it is also possible that 'Maggie's' father, Sir Charles Brodie Locock, a barrister at Lincoln's Inn who practised as an equity draftsman and conveyancer, had also been acquainted with Robert. But whatever the circumstances of their first encounter, Montie and Maggie were married at *St John's Church, Southwick Crescent*, on the 27th December, 1893, curiously, the same day and month of Robert's death. Perhaps this is another clue to the extraordinary reverence Montie bestowed upon his father.

By this time, Montie was already in his fortieth year whereas 'Maggie' was nineteen years his junior but the following examples of verse sent from one to the other in the autumnal months of 1893 leave a delightful impression of their romance as well as an indication of their taste in literature:

'Mystical, more than magical, is that communing of Soul with Soul both looking hereonward!
Here properly, Soul first speaks with Soul.'

Thomas Carlyle

'Measure thy life by loss instead of gain,
Not by the comic drunk, but the vine poured forth:
For Love's strength standeth in
Love's sacrifice,
And whoso suffers most hath most to give.'

Hamilton King

'You well might fear – if Love's sole claim
Were to be happy: but true Love
Takes joy as solace, not as aim,
And looks beyond, and looks above,
And sometimes through the bitterness
Of strife first learns to live her higher life…

If then your future life should need
A strength my love can only gain
Through suffering, or my heart be freed
Only by sorrow, from some strain:-
Then you shall give, and I will take
This crown of fire for Love's dear sake.'

A.Proctor

'One Hope within two Wills!
One Will beneath two overshadowing minds!
One Life, one Death,
One Heaven, one Hell, one Immortality!

Shelley

In many respects, Maggie's background was just as remarkable as that of her *fiancé*. On her paternal side, her grandfather, Sir Charles Locock, Bt, (1799-1875), had experienced an unusually close relationship with Queen Victoria in that he had delivered all nine of her legitimate children. In no way do I use that last adjective disparagingly but, as recent evidence suggests, her relationship with the Scotsman, John Brown, may have given birth to another child not listed amongst the official Royal children and it would be fascinating to know whether Charles, her First Physician-Accoucheur, had been present at that delivery. Furthermore, not only did he act as obstetrician to the Queen's ladies-in-waiting – on one of these occasions, he had to be quarantined at Windsor Castle due to an outbreak of scarlet fever and wrote pages of comic verse to his sisters in order to relieve the boredom – but he also delivered the only son of Empress Eugenie and Napoleon III, the Prince Imperial, *and* selected his nanny! Unfortunately, however, Charles didn't live long enough to persuade the Prince not to join the campaign against Cetshwayo in the Zulu War where he was killed in an ambush in May, 1879.

Another fascinating biography could doubtless be written on the Locock family so I won't indulge the reader in this one apart from adding a brief outline of the first baronet's career with an impression of his personality. Born in Northampton, the son of Henry Locock and Susannah Smyth, Charles studied Medicine at Edinburgh. Like so many eminent physicians educated in Scotland, he travelled to London to establish his career and, for three years, was the resident private pupil of Sir Benjamin Brodie who became Serjeant-Surgeon to the Queen. As an obstetric physician, he quickly established the most successful practice in London and, in 1836, not only became a Fellow of *London University* but also a Fellow of the *Royal College of Physicians* whose Council he was a member of between 1840 and 1842. In 1840, he was chosen from amongst many applicants to be Queen Victoria's First Physician-Accoucheur on the advice of Sir James Clarke, former physician to King Leopold and the Queen's mother, the Duchess of Kent. And in 1857, he was created a baronet in recognition of his services to the Queen, having previously declined the honour in 1840. She also wanted to make him an Earl but, strange as it may seem today, when honours are two a penny, he resisted this offer on the grounds that he feared he would not be able to live up to it despite the fact that his line of ascent could be traced far beyond King Edward I and Eleanor of Castile to the Irish chieftain, Efdchaidh Fedlech, in 14BC! At the time, *Punch* wittily declared that had he accepted this accolade, a fitting title for him would have been 'Lord Deliver-Us!'

Sir Charles, still referred to as 'the old boy' by his existing descendants, also became President of the *Royal Medical and Chirurgical Society* in 1857 before being elected a Fellow of the *Royal Society* in 1864. He resided at *Binstead Lodge*, Ryde, on the Isle of Wight and unsuccessfully contested the parliamentary seat for the island as a Conservative candidate in 1865. His home was only a few miles from Queen Victoria's at *Osborne* and the following passage from his obituary in the *Isle of Wight Observer* adds substance to their mutual high regard for one another:

'For three years Sir Charles' health has been shattered and, during the last twelve months, he has been so extremely feeble that he was unable to receive those friends it had always been his delight to meet. In the course of last week, a great change for the worst was perceptible and her Majesty, as we stated last week, drove over to Binstead on Wednesday to inquire personally after his health, she having always valued him highly as an esteemed friend who had given repeated proofs of his skill and devotion as her physician-accoucheur. The accounts which have reached us of that interview are very touching. Her Majesty went into the chamber where her old friend was lying but he was so ill that he did not recognise her. This, together with the ravages which long illness had made upon him, so affected her Majesty that we hear she burst into tears. Sir Charles, however, recovered consciousness shortly afterwards and, ere her Majesty quitted the room, gathered enough strength to say, 'God bless your Majesty.' And, after she left him, he seemed much better.'

Furthermore, this inventory of some of the family heirlooms bequeathed to his son, Sir Charles Brodie Locock, and listed in the latter's Will, testifies to the esteem in which he was held by other members of the Royal Court. Sadly, these heirlooms had to be auctioned at *Sotheby's* shortly after the premature death of the third baronet's son, Charles Bardolf, in 1959:

'The Will of the late Sir Charles Brodie Locock, who died on January 9th, has been proved with a value of £177, 675. The testator makes heirlooms of the silver table ornaments given to his father, the late Sir Charles Locock, M.D., by the Queen, the gold snuff-boxes by the Emperor Napoleon III, the Sevres china vases and Sevres cups with portraits of the Empress Eugenie and the Prince Imperial by Napoleon III, the Berlin china vases and a bust of the Empress Frederick by the Emperor Frederick, the bronzed clock by the Princess Alice of Hesse, and the bust of Sir Charles by Behnes.'

The first baronet's obituary in the *Medical News* reads:

'If Sir Charles Locock made no important additions to the literature of medicine, his influence was abundantly felt by those who came into contact with him in professional life...His remedies were direct and simple and his whole manner was that of a man who feels just confidence in himself and inspires it in others...He was a plain-speaking, thoroughly independent man, whose advice was sought in all kinds of contingencies by a large number of persons of the highest rank...As a *raconteur*, he was unrivalled; his stories were of the raciest and his aptitude at retort unsurpassed. His great repute had induced certain vendors of quack medicine to advertise cough lozenges under the title of 'Locock's Pulmonic Wafers' or 'Locock's Cough Lozenges.' This, of course, caused him some annoyance. One morning, he met the Duke of Wellington in Hyde Park who said, 'Locock, I have a bad headache from taking your damned lozenges.' 'Well,' said Sir Charles, 'I might as well say that I am lamed by wearing your damned Wellington boots!' But it was not only the vivacity and anecdote, seasoned with copious pinches of snuff, nor yet the unfailing store of experience whence he could draw material for comfort and precedents of treatment, so much as a conviction of his unflagging kindness, gentleness and consideration which endeared him to a large circle of the highest rank. He was particularly esteemed by the Queen to whom he was a valued and confidential friend...'

Besides being acquainted with the Duke of Wellington, he was also a friend of Charles Dickens and William Wordsworth and the following extract from a letter to his father in 1840 gives a vivid description of the ageing poet:

'We all went on Tuesday to call on Wordsworth. He had written a note to me the day before to say he was coming to call on me and, as Fanny Smyth was mad to see a real Poet, we all went with her. The old man was in a most show-up humour and kept us two hours, insisting on walking over the neighbourhood with us and having by far most of the talk to himself. A niece of his, who is staying with him, he has put under my medical care and is much inclined to be sociable. In general, he does not make acquaintances with families or strangers but Judge Coleridge wrote to him some weeks ago to introduce him to us. His conversation is very interesting, full of beautiful reflection, but his appearance is odd and not very attractive – a thin, pale old man, very bald, with little pig's eyes, a broad-brimmed old white hat and coarse, clumsy shoes and stockings. I am going to see him again today and he invites us to an early tea as often as we like as he dines at two o'clock daily.'

On Maggie's maternal side, her grandfather, Canon Thomas Pitman was something of a legendary figure in Eastbourne where he had been vicar for sixty-two years and had reached the ripe old age of eighty-nine, outliving his wife, Frances Jane Bird, who died as early as 1842, and four of his six children, only one of whom reached the age of fifty. When he succeeded Dr Brodie in 1828, Eastbourne was a tiny village with no more than 2,000 inhabitants who were mainly fishermen and their families but, by 1891, the population had grown to 35,000 and this 'village' had become 'one of the largest and most fashionable watering-places in the kingdom and a formidable rival to Brighton which, in those days, was at the height of its reputation.' Furthermore, when Mr Pitman began his Vicariate at *St Mary's*, he was the only clergyman in the village but, at the time of his death in 1890, there were no less than seven parishes in the district, each with their own staff of clergy.

Described by the Rev Walter Budgen as 'a man of great energy and considerable attainments and one who would have made his mark in any calling,' Thomas Pitman was born in 1801, gained a BA at Wadham College, Oxford, in 1826 and an MA in 1827, and, the following year, took up his post at the parish church of *St Mary's* which he found in a sad state of dilapidation. And, during an interview for the *Eastbourne Gazette* in 1888, he said, 'On my appointment, I found the church in ruins. The pews were falling to pieces while the rafters and beams were being destroyed by dry rot.' But there was considerable opposition to him doing anything about it and it was a while before the restoration began. The following extract is taken from the same interview:

'We had a crowded meeting; people came from every part of Eastbourne. Some were very angry and kept interrupting me and asking how the work was to be done. I told them I should recommend it to be done in oak. Others said, 'How much will it cost and where is the Vicar going to get the money?' At this juncture, a market gardener from Seaside was standing at the door of the vestry and said, 'Mr Vicar, that is a capital work you are undertaking and, if you will take a poor man's offering, I will give you £5 5s.' I immediately availed myself of the happy opportunity and said to an opponent, 'You asked me, sir, where I was going to get the money and now I can answer you. I am going to get it from these gentlemen.' 'Not all,' rejoined the Duke of Devonshire, 'I will give £100,' to which Mr Gilbert added, 'And I will give £100 and my sister, whom you married in this church, would like to give £50.' And, in this way, the difficulty was overcome and the matter put in hand.'

The restoration was indeed a mammoth undertaking and photographs before and after clearly reveal the success of this great enterprise. Amongst a considerable list of repairs and refurbishments, every roof had to be renewed, all the windows restored, many of the buttresses rebuilt, the walls refaced inside and out, the massive tower made safe, the pews replaced and a large Willis organ erected by Messrs Walker of London. (A more expansive list can be found in Budgen's book *Old Eastbourne, Its Church, Its Clergy, Its People*. However, it is worth pointing out that the Canon himself donated the massive brass lectern in 1878, a replica of an ancient lectern at the

Church of Holy Trinity, Coventry, the original lectern of *St Mary's* having been buried during the Civil War for 'safe keeping.') The restoration was begun in 1843 and finally completed in 1871, but for one or two minor adjustments, and the total cost of £5,568 was met by voluntary subscription. And, if that wasn't enough to occupy the Canon, he also decided to build a new vicarage on a site adjoining the Workhouse as he deemed the old Vicarage, 'a small, neat residence in the cottage style,' quite unsuitable. An arrangement was made with the Duke of Devonshire for four acres of land – later, in 1887, the Duke generously gave him another four acres to preserve the open aspect of the Vicarage to the south – and funding was obtained through a loan from *Queen Anne's Bounty* which was paid off in 1888.

During his career, Thomas Pitman witnessed as many as six Bishops of Chichester and could also remember the reigns of three English monarchs prior to Queen Victoria as well as a number of smugglers' tales and the fascinating folklore of Beachy Head. As a preacher, he was most earnest and effective and could not 'tolerate any approach to Rome and her teachings' in the Church's worship. Indeed, this particular doctrine would appear to be borne out by Maggie's description of the 5th November celebrations at *St Mary's Vicarage*, Eastbourne in 1877. She was fifteen at the time and the extract is taken from one of her diaries:

'At 9.15, we went up to the Vicarage to see the bonfire opposite the drawing room window. We saw most beautifully as the Pope and Guy Faukes were burnt together. We had great fun and two of the policemen had tea at the Vicarage while we were there.'

Quite what the Catholic Church would have had to say about that, I can only imagine but the diaries give us a clear impression of Maggie's upbringing which was, by all accounts, very happy. Out of three homes at Ampthill, London and Eastbourne, the one at Eastbourne was undoubtedly the family favourite and it was here that Maggie and her five siblings spent many blissful hours riding, bathing, picnicking and making music together. Not surprisingly, with a grandfather as the local Vicar, the family was also fully involved with the life of the church regularly attending functions, choir practices and the three Sunday services but in no way did this level of commitment seem to dampen the children's enthusiasm for Eastbourne. And it might be worth mentioning here that one of Montie's most significant, and successful, *causes célèbres* in 1906 concerned the grievances of three ladies from Eastbourne who were so impecunious that he refused to accept anything more than a token fee. As we shall see, Montie was a compassionate man with a soft spot for wronged women – remember that he had already written two books on the Law relating to women – but I would like to suggest that his generosity in this particular case was, in no small way, influenced by Maggie's connections with the seaside resort; she may have even been acquainted with the women herself.

Be that as it may, 'full of years and beloved and honoured by all who knew him,' the revered Canon finally passed away on the 13th May, 1890, and no less than four thousand mourners gathered in *Ocklynge Cemetery* to pay their last respects. He was obviously a highly venerated and much-loved man. To commemorate sixty years of his Pastorate, a fund was raised in 1888 for two presentation portraits, one to hang in the Town Hall, the other a gift to the Vicar and his family and the frames for these pictures were cut from one of the old oak beams taken from the church. And, again by public subscription, a building intended as a permanent memorial to him was opened in October, 1892 and named the *Pitman Memorial Institute*; its designated function was to provide rooms for parish meetings, classes, reading and recreation. Interestingly, it was built on the very ground where, sixty-four years previously, Mr and Mrs Pitman had debated whether or not to accept the post. There is also a brass memorial to the Canon behind the Vicar's stall and a tablet in the North aisle dedicated to his sons and daughters including Maggie's mother, Fanny Bird Locock, who passed away in 1889 aged fifty-one.

At the time of their marriage, Maggie and Montie had both lost their parents but the family network was still very strong. In fact, it was so strong that Maggie's closest sister, Eva, had obviously found cause to offer Montie an apology after a holiday in Yorkshire, the ancient seat of the Locock family:

Low Stakesby Hall,
Whitby.
August 19th.

My dear Mon,

I am not going to trouble you with a long letter as this is inside one from Maggie which will take up all your thoughts! But I just want to tell you that I am sorry I was horrid to you while you were here. I could not then congratulate you sincerely but I think I can now; I know how much you are to be congratulated because I know what Maggie has been to me and that speaks well for what she will be to you. The news that you were going to take her away came upon me as a shock and it took me a little while to get over it. She and I have been so much to each other. We have always done everything together and you must understand what a great loss she will be out of my everyday life at home.

However, I can now say that I am truly glad for you. I know that I have given you good reason to dislike me but I hope you will try to like me a little.

Yours very sincerely,

Eva C. Locock

Sadly, Eva died of consumption in 1899 at the age of only twenty-nine. But in the meantime, any rifts that were caused by the engagement must have been quickly displaced by the extensive preparations for the wedding. The fact that the couple received over two hundred gifts gives us some idea of the number of invitations despatched by Maggie's elder sister, Lucy, and the extent of Maggie's trousseau suggests that all four of her, as yet, unmarried sisters would have allocated a large part of their daily schedules to accompanying her on her shopping spree at shops such as *Dickens and Jones*, *Liberty* and *Marshall and Snelgrove*. The following list is by no means exhaustive but gives us a fascinating insight as to what such a bride would have been expected to keep in her wardrobe and how much these items would have cost a century ago:

Dresses

Wedding dress £23.0.0 including lace £34.2.6 & orange blossom £60.0.0
'Going away' dress including fur £11.0.0
Blue dress with black velvet £11.11.0
Tweed (black and red) £3.10.0
Blue meroeil evening dress £11.11.0
Black satin & pink dress £7.17.6
Pink Liberty evening dress £2.5.0
Lace evening dress £3.6.0

Cloaks etc...
'Going away' mantle with fur £8.10.3
Fur cloak £9.19.6
Muff to match £2.12.6
Tweed cape £3.3.0
Mackintosh £1.5.0
Umbrella £0.16.3
White opera cloak £3.7.6
Shawl £0.9.6
Wedding veil £1.5.0

Hats
Best 'Travelling' hat – Ritchie £2.2.0
Brown hat with pink down £2.2.0
Black & pink hat – Emilie £0.15.6

Underclothing

12 every day nightdresses
6 best nightdresses trimmed with real lace
12 every day chemises
3 best chemises with lace
4 evening chemises (2 with lace)
15 pairs of drawers
12 elastic silk & cotton petticoat bodies
3 best petticoat bodies
2 evening petticoat bodies with lace

2 silk petticoats (1 white, 1 coloured)
2 best white evening petticoats
6 white (day) summer petticoats
2 coloured summer petticoats
1 alpaca & silk winter petticoats
7 white flannel petticoats (1 best)
4 red flannel petticoats
3 thick jaegars
2 thin jaegars
6 summer vests
16 prs every day stockings (8 thick, 8 thin)
2 prs silk stockings (1 brown, 1 white)
1 pr blue thread stockings
2 prs stays
2 dressing gowns (1 thick, 1 thin)
2 flannel dressing jackets
1 pink silk jacket
2 prs of slippers to match dressing gowns
3 dozen day handkerchiefs
9 evening handkerchiefs (1 Brussels lace, 2 Valenciennes)
5 prs of evening gloves (3 white, 1 tan, 1 black)
3 prs of day gloves
6 veils (2 brown, 4 black)

Boots & shoes

3 prs of walking boots
2 prs house shoes (1 patent, 1 Oxford)
1pr walking shoes
4 prs evening shoes (1 white, 1 bronze, 1 blue, 1 black)

Boxes

Dress basket £4.12.6
P.& O. trunk £4.0.0
'Visiting' case £1.15.0
Bonnet box £1.16.0
Umbrella case £0.4.11

Total: £271.2.8

Whether Maggie was wearing the diamond pendant given to her by Montie as a wedding present, one can only guess but there can be little doubt that she must have looked stunning in her ivory satin dress draped with *point de gaze* and trimmed with trails of orange blossom. And her train of bridesmaids, all similarly adorned with each one wearing a gold bracelet with a pearl and diamond double heart centre presented to them by the bridegroom, must have surely added the icing to the cake. The service itself was conducted by the Revs Leighton Grane and Hanmer Webb Peploe, one of Montie's brothers-in-law, and the bride was given away by her uncle, Colonel Alfred Herbert Locock, R.E. Then, after a magnificent reception at Gloucester Square, the happy couple set off for their honeymoon in north Italy where they were to spend many future holidays rock-climbing with members of both families. Rock-climbing was fast becoming one of the most popular leisure activities of the day.

Chapter Five

A Unique Figure at the Bar

Despite all the major adjustments to his domestic life, marriage was not going to encroach on Montie's professional life at the Bar. If anything, the love and support of his noble and Christian wife probably gave him additional impetus and the following retrospective account from the *Solicitor's Journal* sheds light on how he was beginning to hone his skills as a barrister and how he seemed to cut something of an independent figure amongst his contemporaries:

'Curiously enough, the contrast between Messrs Bankes and Lush was very striking both in physical characteristics, intellectual idiosyncrasies and style of advocacy. The solid physique, weighty and steady legal equipment and downright style of Mr Eldon Bankes was countered by the slight, supple figure, soft, plausible voice and exceedingly agile method of argumentation which drew instant attention to Mr Montague Lush. The latter was quite a unique figure at the Bar since there was no one else who resembled him at all in the tone and colour, so to speak, of his style in court. That indefinite quality, which we describe as 'personality', he possesses in a most marked degree. As an advocate he is most persuasive; there is just the sort of plaintive ring about his voice and alluring suaveness in his manner which creates a certain sympathy in the mind of the tribunal for the wrongs of the client he is representing. He can contrive at a moment's notice a multiplicity of ingenious arguments, all having an air of sanity and scholarship upon any possible point.'

We shall discover how these 'indefinite' qualities seemed to serve Montie rather better at the Bar than they did at the Bench and also how his career progressed in relation to that of Eldon Bankes. But for now, let me introduce the first of many notable cases which played an important part in building his reputation as a successful leader. The case took place only a few years after his marriage and proved that the rewards of perseverance, and tenacity, were not solely confined to gentlemen like his father. The extract is taken from an obituary written by W.J.B.Odhams:

'I am reminded of a case more than 34 years ago which afforded evidence of the uncertainty of the law and the certainty of Mr Lush, as he then was, when he had once made up his mind upon a legal issue.

The managing director of a newspaper my company was printing, the payments for which had got considerably in arrears, gave us a guarantee in the following terms: 'If you will bring out the present number I will repeat my guarantee to see you are paid in full.' The question in dispute was whether the words referred to the expenses of printing the current number or whether it extended to the debt due in respect of past numbers for which verbal guarantee only had been given. The case turned on whether the Statute of Frauds could be pleaded. Mr Lush appeared for the guarantor. In the Court of Queen's Bench, Mr Justice Collins gave emphatic judgement in our favour. The defendant then took the case to the Court of Appeal where, after reserving judgement, the Master of the Rolls, Mr Justice Lopes, and Lord Justice Rigby unanimously upheld us. Mr Lush, however, was convinced that the four judges' interpretation of the Statute was wrong and persuaded the defendant to take the case to the House of Lords, obtaining leave to do so in *forma pauperis.* Here, four Law Lords, including, if I remember rightly, Lord Davey and Lord James of Hereford, unanimously gave the case against us.'

A successful practice at the Bar was inevitably rewarded by handsome remuneration and, by this time, Montie's income was sufficient to support a new family. He and Maggie were living in *Fitzjohn's Avenue*, Hampstead, and it was there that their first child, Helen Margaret was born in 1895. Then, in two year intervals, came Montague Arthur, Harold Charles and Maurice Hubert. All three of these boys attended *Orley Farm School* at Harrow, a Prep School whose numbers have trebled since those days and which is about to celebrate its 150th anniversary. Arthur and Harold then went to *Westminster School*, as their father had done, while Maurice went to *Harrow*. Maggie then took a break from childbearing until 1908 when she gave birth to Wilfred Robert, otherwise known as 'Bobby', and, three years later, their last child, Violet, was brought into the world. More will be said about their lives later in the chapter but, for now, it might be interesting to note that, just like their parents and grandparents, they were all very short apart from Harold who seems to dwarf everyone in the family photographs!

All the same, size is not everything, as we well know, and what Montie lacked in physical stature, he more than made up for in terms of reputation. In 1901, the year of Queen Victoria's death, he became the Treasurer of *Gray's Inn*, like his father before him, and finally 'took Silk' after twenty-three years as a junior in 1902. By now, he had become a leading authority on questions of commercial law and a blandly pertinacious cross-examiner. And as a King's Counsel, few of his contemporaries equalled him in the volume of his practice. Apparently, he was a master in the delicate art of carrying on as many as four cases simultaneously and it was a common sight to see him rushing from one Court to the next with only the slightest briefing from his junior and a quick sandwich on the hoof. According to one of his biographers: 'Of amazing quickness of perception, he needed no more than a hint from his junior to put him in possession of the situation that had arisen in his absence and a note consisting of a few words enabled him to make exactly the speech that the case required.' Not surprisingly, therefore, his life as a KC was almost absurdly frenetic and since his services were in such great demand, he even turned down the offer of a judgeship at the *Probate, Admiralty and Divorce Division* also in 1902. Interestingly, had he accepted this post, his progress up the judicial ladder might well have led him to sit at the *Court of Appeal* where, ironically, he might have made more of an impression than he did on the *King's Bench*. But, in reality, Montie was in his element at the Bar and, if he had chosen the course on offer, the reputation that he was about to acquire in the public arena as a champion of the sensational *causes célèbres* of his day would surely not have materialised.

Many of these cases stole the headlines and, needless to say, the public interest in his outstanding work quickly snowballed. Since this is a biography and not a Law Journal, it does not fall within my remit to cover all these cases in great depth but I will attempt to cover a cross-section of them by including some of the more, and less, sensational ones as well as some of those which he won or lost.

Firstly, in 1901/1903, there was the case of *Bradley v Carritt* involving litigation over mortgage agreements. The following summary is taken from the *Lords Journals*:

A holder of shares in a tea company mortgaged the shares to secure a loan and agreed to use his best endeavours to secure that 'always thereafter' the mortgagee should have the sale of all the company's teas as broker and, in the event of any of the company's teas being sold otherwise than through the mortgagee, to pay him the amount of commission he would have earned if the teas had been sold through him. The mortgage was paid off and the company afterwards changed their broker. The quondam mortgagee having brought an action against the shareholder for breach of the above agreement:

Held, by Lords MacNaghten, Davey and Robertson that the agreement was not binding and that the action could not be maintained. The decision of the Court of Appeal was reversed.

In the first trial, judgement was entered in favour of the plaintiff, Carritt, who was suing the Bradley brothers for breach of agreement and this was later affirmed by the *Court of Appeal*. However, Montie, who was acting for the Bradleys, managed to persuade the Lords to reverse this decision on the basis that the agreement ceased to be operative when the mortgage was redeemed. This was by no means a sensational case but, nevertheless, was an important one as far as contract law was concerned and was a triumph for Montie.

The next case, on the other hand, stole plenty of headlines in 1904 although, in the distinct absence of witnesses, Montie failed to convince the jury on behalf of his pretty client who was the plaintiff in the action. From the entertaining passage that follows, it is easy enough to see why the case had attracted so much attention but it is also worth noting that Montie's opponent was his most formidable rival, Sir Edward Carson:

JURY DISAGREE

END OF ACTRESS'S BREACH OF PROMISE SUIT

Plaintiff in tears

A little 'scene' between Judge and Counsel

The remarkable breach of promise suit brought by Miss Marian Draughn, a pretty American actress, against Heinrich Thyssen, the son of the German millionaire ironmaster, came to an end last night after occupying Mr Justice Grantham's court for four days. The jury failed to agree on a verdict and they were discharged.

Most of the day had been taken up by the speeches of counsel. Mr Thyssen was in the witness-box for about an hour and then there was a discussion as to whether two witnesses for the defence should be heard who were to speak of Miss Draughn's visiting Hummums Hotel with Mr Philip May. Finally, the judge decided that the evidence was not admissible and Sir Edward Carson proceeded to make a strong attack on the only witness called for the plaintiff – herself. He was followed by Mr Lush, who proceeded to do the same for the only witness for the defence – the defendant, only Mr Lush's attack was perhaps stronger than Sir Edward's. They were both, however, good specimens of forensic indignation.

Mr Justice Grantham summed up – that is he put the plaintiff's case rather more strongly than Mr Lush had done and this because he left out all Mr Lush's adjectives. Sir Edward Carson shifted uneasily in his seat and kept taking voluminous notes whilst that prominent under-jaw of his grew longer and longer. At last, the judge had finished and the jury, after a moment's consultation, decided to leave the box.

Notes between Judge and Jury

By this time it was twenty minutes to five and the crowded court broke up into little groups which chatted together and discussed the possibilities of the verdict. Having listened to the judge's summing-up, Miss Draughn looked radiant and she chatted confidently with her solicitor, Mr Arthur Newton. The judge wrote letters while the audience waited.

This waiting time went on exactly for one hour when the juryman's bell rung and a rustle of anticipation ran through the court. It was only a message for the judge, however. After reading it, Sir William handed over the note to both counsel who glanced over it and returned it to the judge. In doing this, Sir Edward said: 'The answer is no, my Lord.'

The note was an inquiry as to whether the parties would accept a verdict of the majority of the jury.

This led to renewed speculations. The plaintiff's friends began to look concerned. Visions on the one side of a £5,000 verdict began to fade away and the desirability or not of moving for a new trial ceased to be a question of interest to the defendant and his friends. Then the jurymen's bell rang again and a long slip of blue paper was brought up to the judge.

Mr Justice Grantham read it and proceeded to write something in reply. Sir Edward Carson jumped up and said, 'May we hear what the jury have to say, my Lord?'
'No, you may not, Sir Edward,' was the judge's reply.
'But I always thought that a judge and jury had to say what they had to say in open court, my Lord?'
'I have never heard that suggested before,' said Sir William, and he continued writing his message to the jury.
Sir Edward Carson flounced back into his seat, his face as black as thunder. 'Fancy a judge writing private letters to a jury while they are considering their verdict,' he jerked out in a very audible 'aside.'

Miss Draughn weeps

Finally, at five minutes past six, having been away for an hour and twenty-five minutes, the jury once more filed into their box.

'Gentlemen of the jury, are you agreed on your verdict?' inquired the associate.
'We are not,' replied the foreman.
Miss Draughn burst into tears.
'Is there no chance of your agreeing?' said the judge.
'No, my lord, not the slightest,' replied the foreman of the jury. 'We have argued the matter from all points and we are quite convinced that there is no chance of our coming to an agreement.'
'I am very sorry to hear it,' was the judge's comment, 'especially on account of the parties concerned. But as you say there is no chance of agreeing, I have no alternative but to discharge you.' And then the court broke up, leaving the case undecided.

The earlier proceedings were somewhat uninteresting, not to say dull. Mr Thyssen went into the box for the conclusion of his cross-examination and was at once taken in hand by Mr Lush. Mr Thyssen furnished counsel with a card giving the address of his father's representative in London. Then followed a discussion as to Mr Thyssen's business relations with his father.
'Have you any interest in your father's business?' asked Mr Lush.
'Certainly,' said the defendant.
'Are you a partner?'
'No.'
'Then what are you?'

His 'interest'

'I am his son,' said Mr Thyssen, amid a burst of laughter.

Mr Thyssen went on to say that his family had offered to help in the case but he refused to accept anything. 'I did not mean to be blackmailed,' he said.
'We shall see about the blackmail when we get a little further,' replied Mr Lush.

A discussion followed between counsel and defendant as to the reason why the latter would not sign an agreement to pay Miss Draughn £5 a week. Again and again, he replied, 'Because I didn't want to,' amid laughter.

'Did you want to keep the knowledge of it from your wife?'
'My wife knew all about it.'

Mr Lush pressed Mr Thyssen about the marriage laws of Germany. Were not secret marriages impossible, seeing that the consent of the parents was necessary? Mr Thyssen did not think so when the parties were over age.
'What is the blackmail you complain of?' asked Mr Lush.
'How shall I translate it?' asked the defendant. 'She was making an attempt to get money under false pretences.'
'Trying to get money because you failed to carry out your promise to marry her?'
'I never promised to marry her.'

Tired of it

'I have heard you say that until I am blue in the face,' said Mr Lush.
Sir Edward Carson: 'I dare say you are!' (laughter)
'About the £600 you borrowed of Miss Draughn,' said Mr Lush. 'You invested it in shares for her?'
'Yes.'
'And they went up to three or four times their original value?'
'They ought to have done but they did not.' (laughter)

Sir Edward Carson put a few questions in re-examination of the defendant. It was a pure invention to say that he ever went under a false name. He had no desire to escape pecuniary liability in Germany should the trial go against him.
'Rightly or wrongly, did you think it made a difference when you were charged with seduction under a promise of marriage?'
'Yes, I did.'
'And you refused to make any settlement so long as these charges were being held over you?'
'Yes. When I speak of extortion, I mean getting money out of me by making a claim that I promised to marry her and, under that promise, seduced her.'

Mr Thyssen went on to say that his father had joined the Steel Combine in Germany three years ago.

The judge: 'What the Americans call a Trust.'
Sir Edward Carson: 'There is always a difficulty about the word 'Trust' so they use the word 'Combine.' It means the same thing.'

When the defendant left the box, Sir Edward desired to put a cabman, who drove Miss Draughn to the Hummums Hotel, and the hall porter of that hotel in the box. His aim was, he said, to prove that Mr May was with her there. Mr Lush said he should be ready to accept the challenge if time were given him to bring further evidence but the judge held that the evidence was not admissible.

Sir Edward then rose to sum up for his client. He said that the defendant's case was that the plaintiff agreed to be his mistress and that he agreed to pay her for doing so. That might be a nasty story to tell in a court of justice but he was bound to remind him that such conduct gives no ground of action in such courts. Such things did happen in the world although, in courts of justice, they sometimes pretended to know nothing about them.

Had any promise been made and, if so, was that promise corroborated? Sir Edward went through the evidence and the letters and contended that the answer to both questions was in the negative. It was claimed that Miss Draughn was an innocent, straight, and honourable girl before she met Mr Thyssen. Then what about Mr May and Mr Ansell? asked Sir Edward. He concluded by asking the jury to dismiss all question of sentiment from their minds.

Mr Lush replied for the plaintiff. He asked the jury to remember the mental torture through which his client had had to pass. For six weeks, the defendant, with all the power which money gave him, strove to rake up accusations against the woman he had wronged and all that could be found was that two men, who were now dead, had been friends – and nothing else – of Miss Draughn's.

Counsel, in conclusion, declared that the defendant was a man without a spark of honour who had put himself outside the pale of decent society by his conduct towards this lady.

Whilst Mr Lush was speaking, the Chancellor of the Exchequer came on to the bench and sat down beside the judge for a few minutes. Mr Asquith heard the end of Mr Lush's slashing attack on the defendant.

The judge commenced to sum up at four o'clock. He described the case as one of the most difficult that had ever come before his Court. On reviewing the evidence, his Lordship said that it had been proved on the whole that there had been a promise of marriage and he thought that nothing had been brought forward against Miss Draughn's moral character. She had agreed to accept an allowance from Mr Thyssen after her engagement to him until arrangements could be made to obtain the consent of the defendant's father. He did not regard this as an out-of-the-way arrangement.

The following year found Montie involved with three trade union actions, the most famous of which was the case of the *Denaby Collieries v the Yorkshire Miners Association*. Various pay disputes had led to a miners' strike which was deemed unlawful because their contracts stipulated that they were not entitled to stop working prior to the end of fourteen days' notice. The Association was well aware of these terms of employment and tried to get the men back to work. Nevertheless, matters were further complicated because, in 1901, the Home Secretary had issued new regulations in regard to timbering so some of the miners had signed one contract and some another and, when the longer serving men were asked to sign the new contract, they refused. So the strike continued and the employers were suing the union for damages. The first judgement was entered in favour of the employers, represented by Montie and Bankes. However, this judgement was reversed by the *Court of Appeal*, in which the *Sheffield Telegraph* accredited Montie's argument with 'one of the ablest ever heard' in that particular court, and the reversal was then affirmed in the *House of Lords* in May, 1906, on the basis that the union could not be held liable for the actions carried out by the leaders of the strike whom it had not authorised. Certainly, the issue caused quite a stir at the time so I was not surprised to discover the following passage written by one of Montie's literary admirers under the pseudonym of LEX:

To the Memory of 'The Bag Dirt Question'

Which hatched in the Bowels of the Earth
First saw light at Cadeby A.D.1896
And was christened 'Top Cutting.'
In the next year it received a rude shock
At Doncaster County Court
And altered its name as above.
For the next four years it maintained
A spasmodic existence:
And in February,1901, the Men's Arbitrators priced it
At a half penny.
On St Valentine's day, 1902,
It received another blow
At the same County Court
But, galvanized into a mock vitality,
In the month of June in the same year
By Trade Union Agitators,
It formed a pretext for a strike
Of unprecedented magnitude.
Under the masterly hand of Rufus Isaacs
It acquired in the Law Courts
A semblance of substantial reality:-
But blown up by Montague Lush,
Amidst the plaintive moans of Atherley Jones,
It collapsed like a house of cards
And was finally laid to rest
By Lawrance J. and a Special Jury
On Monday 8th February, 1904.

But we have the advantage of hindsight. Despite Montie's efforts to conquer the beast that 'hatched' at Cadeby, it still had the legs to carry it to the *House of Lords*.

Charles Montague Lush

Maggie Lush (née Margaret Abbie Locock)
with her eldest daughter and son, Helen and Montague Arthur, nanny
and dog, Punch, c.1905

1906 was a particularly busy year for Montie. He was now reaching the peak of his career as a leader but a moving letter from his widowed sister, Elizabeth Watkin Williams, provides us with the first real indication that he was overstretching himself:

8, Aberdeen Cottages,
Stanmore.
Jan 5. 1906.

My dearest Mon,

I meant in any case to have sent you a word of my most loving admiration today for your brave holding not only on all your duties but also on every most minute detail of care for others in all your human heart break and worn condition of nerves from the terrible, practical strain on them. It struck me immensely in proof of how far you had advanced and of how it proves that 'whatever the pruning knife may be, it is not the knife that prunes, but the Father's hand.' I do trust that now you are over anxious and that Dr Taylor will say that these are the very difficulties he meant to warn you of; but however that may be, I am <u>very</u> sure that your lives prove that you and Margaret are in the Father's loving care and that neither faith nor comfort will fail you in need. While I hope and believe that the new born year will bring you both a rich return of all your good work, I will quote the words in 'Wisdom' I referred to because I think that too often we dwell on our own and not in 'the dear one's park' in such overwhelming sorrow: 'Yea, speedily was he taken away, lest that wickedness should alter his understanding, or *devil* beguile his soul...' Solomon. 4.11. But I pray that you and Margaret will work out towards the higher life, which means perfection, together for many years yet as I truly believe you will.

Bless you for your kind putting me off today and it makes me happy in the confidence that you <u>will</u> send for me when I, in the least degree, can help you. You have given me new faith and I hope towards the higher life. I am more than ever, dear Mon, your truly loving and grateful sister.

Elizabeth Watkin Williams.

All the same, despite the concerns of his sister, and presumably those of his doctor, he continued to represent his clients in notable cases such as *Paquin v Beauclerk*, *Modera v Barttelot* and *Dealtry v the Countess of Aberdeen*. But, despite his renowned courtesy towards the Bench, his patience was evidently beginning to wear a little thin in this last case with both his opponent and the judge who were constantly interrupting his eloquent arguments:

Lord Justice Vaughan Williams: You had better go on with your narrative, Mr Lush.
Mr Lush: I intend to do so, your Lordship, if I am not interrupted either by my learned friend or by...
Vaughan Williams, LJ: I notice that you did not finish your sentence, Mr Lush.
Mr Lush: Perhaps I may be allowed to do so on another occasion, your Lordship.

And the writer for the *Law Journal*, who was seemingly sympathetic towards Montie's dilemma, concludes his account with an amusing but relevant quote from the Lord Chief Justice:

'The absolutely silent judge is one of the most unpleasant judges to practise before because the advocate never knows what is in his mind. The garrulous judge, on the other hand, is an intolerable nuisance because he lengthens the proceedings and diverts attention from the points in the mind of the advocate.'

There are no prizes for guessing into which category Lord Justice Vaughan Williams might have belonged. However, he was not presiding over the next case which must have been one of the most precious jewels in Montie's professional necklace and which attracted a great deal of media attention. As previously mentioned, Maggie had family connections with Eastbourne; moreover, Montie's own links with the *Mission Hall* must have surely endowed him with more than an ordinary degree of compassion for the plight of poor women and especially for those who had been wronged in the eyes of the Law. The best summary of this case that I have found comes from the retrospective pen of W.J. Wenham, the same solicitor/bard who had venerated Montie through his prose on the *Bag Dirt Question*. This letter was written to Montague Arthur shortly after Montie's death and revealed the same address found on the poems signed LEX thereby disclosing the true identity of the bard:

5, Gray's Inn Square,
June 30, 1930

Dear Sir,

...Since you bear his name, may I be permitted to tell you why, to my last day, I shall hold his memory more sacred than that of any other judge or advocate at the English Bar.

In my youth I was privileged to instruct him, with Sir F. Newbolt, Junior, for the Plaintiffs in the great case of Jewell v. Oetzmann. It was a case where three poor ladies – lodginghouse keepers in Eastbourne – had been brought wholly to ruin by the sack and looting by the Defendants of six big houses in Eastbourne. All their savings and hard work for years were gone and I recall that I took my instruction by candlelight in their ruined house since even the gas fittings had been swept away.

My study of the nobler doctrines of the Common Law induced me to believe that, if I could once get the case into Court, such an outrage must sufficiently be vindicated and, after two long years of hard fighting in which I imperilled my own slender resources, I got it there. Then came the question of the leader. Newbolt, who was as keenly impressed as myself with the moral aspect of the case, kindly undertook to lay the facts before your noble father who was then at the very height of his forensic career in the House of Lords, Court of Appeal, and, in fact, in every great case of the day.

As the result of your late father's impression of the case, and despite the immense work and bulk of papers in it, he caused his clerk to accept the four briefs marked with a ludicrously low fee since the ladies had practically no means; in fact, one might almost say a nominal fee. It was the most chivalrous and knightly action within my experience of the Bar of England.

Never shall I forget the intensity of the late judge's surprise and indignation when the indubitable facts of the case were disclosed to him in consultation; never shall I forget that grave, beautiful silvery voice with quiet confidence assuring the Plaintiffs, within five minutes of meeting them for the first time, that their wrongs could only, and should beyond all doubt, be assuaged not in terms of hundreds but of thousands of pounds of damages. Newbolt, I recall, after the ladies had gone, mildly ventured to enquire whether, as to the measure of damages, his learned leader might not be too optimistic. The late judge then, seemingly surprised at Newbolt's query, firmly asseverated his prediction which subsequently was realised.

The case coming on before the late Mr Justice Bucknill, and a Special Jury, Sir Montague rose in a crowded Court and, in terms of noble but restrained emotion, laid bare my Clients' heavy wrongs. He spoke for three hours and, when he sat down in an electric atmosphere, I knew that the case was won.

Vauvenargues said that 'great thoughts come from the heart' and that piece of matchless advocacy came (as everyone knowing him realised) red hot from the warm and noble heart which now lies stilled for ever.

The rest need scarcely be set down. Everything had been accomplished by that marvellous speech which pulsed with sincerity and humanity. That, thereafter, the battle raged for sixteen days with ever increasing success for my Clients; that dear old H.F. Dickens, K.C., son of the illustrious novelist, on the other side, did everything mortally possible to stem the tide of human emotion which had set in from your father's eloquence; that Judge Bucknill expressed his increasing sense of the gravity of the Defendant's conduct; all these were minutiae. Sir Montague's prediction came true; the Defendants ultimately sought for terms to avoid the verdict of the Jury and, finally, Mr Acland and Mr Newbolt struck out a settlement for £3,000 damages with all costs...

I am, Sir,

Yours sincerely,

W.J.Wenham.

Not surprisingly, this case was dubbed 'The Furniture Case' and, apparently, Judge Bucknill 'was particularly amused by the evidence of Mrs Jewell who spoke with a broad West Country accent' himself being an eminent Devonian. Meanwhile, Montie and Maggie probably found the following account in the *Eastbourne Gazette* quite a talking point:

'Miss Ellen Jewell shed tears, and so did her aged mother who tottered blindly into the crowded corridor, and was held up by sympathising friends. A chorus of congratulations soon dried the tears of Miss Ellen who expressed, more or less publicly, her desire to embrace Mr Lush, KC who had fought so staunch a battle for her and the historic household of Grand Parade. Miss Ellen said that she was going to work harder than ever to popularise her elegant boarding-house business. She is assured that her old friends and many, many new ones will rally round her and that the 1906 summer season will be the brightest she has seen for a good many years.'

If that wasn't enough excitement for 1906, there was one more case which didn't attract quite the same headlines but which was, nonetheless, highly significant because the defendant was none other than Lord Justice Fletcher Moulton himself whom Montie was now acting against. Broadly speaking, Moulton was trustee of his late wife's estate and had sought to be compensated for the maintenance of his stepchildren, a strategy which one of the children, Mrs Kenneth Grahame, was now contesting. At the first hearing, the judge ruled that reimbursement for their maintenance was perfectly reasonable but, at the *Court of Appeal*, this judgement was reversed partly on the grounds that the so-called verbal agreement made between Moulton and the children relating to this maintenance was flatly denied by them and partly because the children had more than earned their keep by keeping house for their stepfather in the manner required by the status of his profession. The appeal was therefore allowed by the Master of the Rolls, Lord Justice Collins, with costs in both courts and Montie had won the day. And, besides the status of the respondent, this was no mean feat especially since Montie's principal opponent, Rufus Isaacs, KC, who was one of the leading Goliaths of the day, was currently holding the upper hand in the Denaby case!

In 1909, Montie was involved in two famous industrial disputes: *Rhondda Urban Council v Taff Vale Railway Company* and *E. Hulton and Company v Artemus Jones*. The first of these concerned obligations over the width of roads to and over bridges and Montie was successful on behalf of the District Council in getting the decision of the *Court of Appeal* reversed in the *House of Lords*. And the second concerned a libel action against a newspaper which had portrayed a fictitious person with the same name as the respondent in an 'unflattering light'; again, Montie was successful on behalf of the respondent by ensuring that the original judgement for substantial damages was confirmed by the Lords.

However, while he was engaged in the famous Townshend inquiry and the case of *Wyler v Lewis* in 1910, the year when George V came to the throne, rumours were beginning to circulate that Mr Lewis might have to find himself another barrister since Montie was widely tipped for a seat on the *King's Bench*. Evidently, there was a great deal of truth in these rumours:

Esher House,
Esher.
Oct. 3, 1910

My dear Judge,

On my way from Paris I learned the good news that you had been elevated. The little bird whose whispers I divulged to you was not far wrong when it said that Bankes and you were to be made judges. I was disappointed not to see you both appointed as the two additional judges. However, better late than never. I was tremendously pleased to see the announcement and I congratulate you most heartily upon the appointment which I know will be as popular as it is well deserved. I rejoice in it all the more as it has fallen upon a friend from whom I have always received much kindness and for whom, if you will allow me to say so, I cherish a great regard. We have fought many battles together on the same side and against each other and the memory of them all is not only pleasant but instructive. I wish you every happiness in your new sphere of utility; long may you remain there to the delight of your friends and the Bar in general and to the great benefit of all those who are unfortunate enough to commit the folly of going to law. I am always sorry for people who go to law but happy will those be who get their cases tried before you. I hope soon to see you arrayed in all your glory.

Yours most sincerely,

F.P.Schiller.

And the news was quick to spread. Amongst the congratulations were the following letters:

Lombarden,
Limpsfield,
Surrey.
Sept 29th, 1910

My darling Maggie,

How very delightful and exciting this piece of news is – we are so pleased! It is splendid! I am so glad to think that Montie will not now have to work quite so hard (at least I hope not) though of course the responsibility is very great. We are so excited about it and have sent off a telegram which I hope will reach you one of the first!

You will have to give up all your wicked little ways now you are the wife of a Judge!

Morton joins with me in warmest congratulations to you both.

Much love darling
from your loving sister
Dora

3, King's Bench Walk, North Temple.
30th Sept, 1910

My dear Lush,

This is indeed good news but it makes me feel old. What we shall do without you I know not. I shall miss your cheery friendship dreadfully as there is now between us that great gulf of majesty. Still, I may benefit as, of course, you will always decide in my favour. That you will decide, and wisely, I am confident and with costs – no weakness to save the other man's face. No nonsense now. We must have the best and only the best from you.

As you have been a great advocate, you will also be a great judge. *felix opportunitate.* I congratulate you and, above all, the country. Thank heaven no politics! How I long to be led by you again. Life is like that.

Ever yours,

Frank Newbolt
(a North-Eastern Circuit Judge – hooray!)

178, Cromwell Road,
S.W.
30th Sept.1910.

Dear Mr Lush,

I trust my congratulations on your appointment as Judge of the High Court may not be out of place, and that you will accept them as an expression of my great personal pleasure. Amongst my earliest memories of the Law Courts is that of often lingering to listen to your arguments for pure intellectual enjoyment whenever you had a fighting case on; a temptation I have yielded to at intervals ever since…It has been my good fortune to have had act for me quite a large number of counsel who are now on the Bench or hold life appointments but your career has fascinated me, quite apart from any personal intercourse. I look forward to some day seeing you sit in that centre-seat in Appeal Court 1 whence I have so often heard Lord Esher battling against your arguments, only to be convinced, sometimes very unwillingly, in the end.

Yours sincerely,

Frederic Hudson.

The Holt,
Harrow Weald.
6th Oct. 1910

Dear Lady Lush,

My wife went to London very early or would be joining in my congratulations. Here is a short story giving proof of what is thought of Sir Montague's great power if such proof were needed! At the Club the other day, a leading solicitor said to me, 'Thank Heaven Lush has been made a Judge; now we can never have him against us anymore.'

Anon

And amongst some of the more enlightening tributes:

Westminster Gazette:

'By the appointment of Mr Montague Lush, KC to the vacancy of the King's Bench, caused by the retirement of Mr Justice Jelf, another golfing zealot has become a judge. However, the report that Mr A.J.Balfour is revising the rules of golf is denied and the suggestion that the Lord Chief Justice has appointed a rota, consisting of himself and Judges Lawrence, Crutton, and Lush, to sit as a divisional court to hear Welsh and English golfing appeals, is equally void of foundation.

In Scotland, I believe, a new judge sits *pro forma* to hear some simple motion in the presence of the other judges and thereupon, having proved himself efficient, he is called to the Bench. The function is a sort of public examination of fitness. Had this practice been pursued in England, Grantham and Bucknill would have heard a motion on the rules of the Jockey Club, the Lord Chief Justice one on the rules of the Amateur Athletic Association and Eldon Bankes would have considered the laws of the Amateur Rowing Association. Under this practice, the appointment of Mr Justice Lush would have been most opportune. The Royal and Ancient Golf Club has just held its general meeting and has passed new rules so the new judge might have had to consider either the nature of a golf club or the precise effect of the new rule as to lifting and teeing a ball in stroke play. As to the latter rule, it is about as mysterious as some of the statutes relating to copyright. Perhaps Scrutton, J. might employ his spare time and write a thesis thereon. In the Vacation Court, he stated that he granted leave to serve some notice of motion just after he had done a lovely drive and before the final putt. Meanwhile, an irreverent junior wondered whether his partner was badly bunkered or hunting for a sliced ball.'

Liverpool Post:

'Mr Justice Lush comes of a judicial stock, has a portentous knowledge of law, a most engaging manner, a florid complexion, and is a capital fellow. He once observed that he had been entitled to write his book, 'The Law of Husband and Wife,' because he had never had an angry word with his own wife.'

Leeds Mercury:

'For many years, his practice has flourished like the proverbial bay tree and he is rather an exception in that he has done but little circuit work, his London cases occupying most of his time. With a voice of peculiarly melodious quality, Mr Lush combined a power of onslaught equal to that of Mr Avory. His eyes gleaming with indignation, he almost threw himself on his victim.'

Some other excerpts:

'When most dangerous he assumes a manner of seeming carelessness and will lead a witness along on a string of innocent questions before suddenly launching a vital question which takes his witness quite by surprise...He enjoyed so large a practice at the junior Bar that he could not afford to take silk until eight years ago. Since then, he has always been in the running for a judgeship...As Counsel, he was an extremely rapid speaker and his volubility was always something to wonder at. On the Bench he will probably be more deliberate and will also shed the little habit of twisting a piece of red tape round his finger as an 'aid to advocacy' in a particularly knotty case...He was called to the Bar at Gray's Inn thirty-one years ago and, in that learned society, the appointment will be especially welcomed for it is a remarkable fact that, for several years, this Inn of Court has not had a member who was a Judge of the High Court...'

This last sentence couldn't have been more accurate and the *Westminster Gazette* again reports:

'The Hon Mr Justice Lush, who is a Bencher of Gray's Inn, has been presented by some of the barristers of that society with a silver loving-cup of the period of Charles II, a silver salver and an address on the occasion of his appointment as a Judge of His Majesty's High Court of Justice. The presentation was made in the large Pension Chamber at Gray's Inn on Monday last. The proceedings were quite informal. The senior barrister present made the presentation and Mr Justice Lush, in expressing his thanks, asked to be allowed to accept the gifts as tokens of personal regard and affection from fellow-members of the Bar of Gray's Inn.'

The cup bears the inscription, 'Presented to the Honourable Sir Charles Montague Lush, in token of sincere regard and respect by some brother barristers of the Society of Gray's Inn, as a memento of the 6th October, 1910,' and is now the property of that Inn along with an oil painting of Montie by Dorofield Hardy presented by his brother, Herbert, in 1932.

The judge whom Montie was succeeding was Sir Arthur Jelf who had resigned his post. Sir Arthur was the son of the Rev Richard Jelf, a Principal of *King's College*, London, and had been educated at *Eton* and *Christchurch*, Oxford. As an advocate, he had been highly successful, exhibiting a high degree of shrewdness and practical common sense together with a breezy contempt for red tape. (Hopefully, not the same red tape that Montie was prone to wrapping round his little finger!) And, as a judge, he had a reputation for 'getting to the heart of things with the least possible delay' even though some of his methods were deemed to be rather unconventional at that time; for instance, a year or so before he retired, he visited a music hall for the purpose of seeing for himself two 'turns' which were the subject of the litigation before him. By all accounts, he was certainly quite a character and, at a luncheon at *Gray's Inn* in May, 1907, when he was sitting next to Maggie, he must have provided her with plenty of stimulating conversation. The following extract sheds further light on some of his little eccentricities:

'A somewhat grimly amusing story is told of Mr Justice Jelf when he was Recorder. A prisoner before him began to weep in a most distressing manner.
'Why do you weep?' said Mr Jelf.
'Oh, my Lord, my dear Lord,' came the tearful answer. 'I have never, never been to prison before.'
'Don't cry, prisoner at the Bar,' was the cheerful response. 'I am going to send you there right now!"

On the 12th October, 1910, Montie, Eldon Bankes, Horrace Avory and Thomas Horridge were knighted by George V at *Marlborough House*. Bankes, a former Oxford blue and great leader at the Common Law Bar, was considered 'the personification of good form' who, perhaps, 'did not possess the erudition of a Danckwerts or the infinite plausibility of a Lush but always drove his case well home.' Avory, on the other hand, was one of the greatest criminal lawyers of the day whose manner was not so attractive but, nevertheless, 'had a way of getting to the heart of things which, in the end, conquered many a hostile jury.' And Horridge, a man who largely owed his elevation to the House of Commons, was remembered for 'giving Mr

Balfour a sound beating' in the East Manchester elections of 1906.

Later that same morning, and despite the pouring rain, a large gathering of spectators formed outside *Westminster Abbey* to await the arrival of the judges in their closed carriages for the ceremony at noon, the fourteenth of its kind to have taken place at the Abbey since 1897 and which marked the opening of the legal year. Standing in the nave were the Lord Chancellor, the Deputy Serjeant-at-Arms with the mace, and a large assembly of county-court judges, barristers and registrars. And once the judges had arrived, the Dean of Westminster led the procession up the aisle, headed by the choir and clergy. The choral service lasted for about half an hour and included two psalms and Wesley's anthem *Ascribe unto the Lord.* After the final hymn, 'O God, our help in ages past,' the blessing was pronounced by the Dean and the judges then adjourned to the House of Lords where they enjoyed the hospitality of the Lord Chancellor.

It was still raining when the judges approached the *Royal Courts of Justice* for the traditional opening ceremony at two o'clock. Nevertheless, there was another considerable crowd of people waiting outside to greet them and the central hall was packed with spectators not only on the ground floor but also on the balconies and stairways. And most of the seats in the jury-box in court were occupied by the judges' wives, a spectacle which must have provided a refreshing change from the customary occupants! Each of the judges, wearing his full regalia, was then sworn-in in the presence of the Lord Chief Justice and the majority of the judges of the *King's Bench Division*, all resplendent in their scarlet robes and full-bottomed wigs. Mr Justice Bankes was the first to take the oath and was followed, in turn, by Mr Justice Avory, Mr Justice Horridge and Mr Justice Lush. And what a memorable day it must have been!

Despite what Schiller had said in his letter, two of the new judgeships were, in fact, additional appointments in an effort to reduce the rapidly increasing backlog of cases which had become a serious problem. From the newspaper cuttings, it was evident that the onus was on all of the new judges to push the cases through the courts as quickly as possible and, true to form, Montie was off to a flying start:

'Mr Justice Lush sat for the first time in open court as a judge of the King's Bench Division and greatly impressed all who sat before him with the way he has of getting through the work. Today, he ran through a quartet of common jury cases in excellent time and was ready for more work by the time the other judges were still in the middle of their list. Of course, it may have been a pure piece of luck. Anyway, Mr Justice Lush was able to give very welcome aid to Mr Justice Coleridge who had one of those terrible 'sticking' cases and in whose court the look-out for other patiently-waiting litigants was very poor. In spite of his smallness of stature, Mr Justice Lush makes a dignified judicial figure on the bench.'

'Some nice new Daniels come to judgement: the polished Avory, the h'affable Horridge, the blossoming Bankes, and the blushing Lush.'

Punch, 12th October, 1910

Chapter Six

The Little Man with a Big Reputation

1911 must have also been a significant year for Montie in many respects. Not only was he created an Honorary Fellow of *Trinity Hall*, Cambridge, but also, on the 2nd March, he gave a well-received address at the first meeting of the *Chester and North Wales Law Clerks' Society*. The following extract from the minutes embodies his warm sentiments for Wales and the Welsh people as well as underlining his deep reverence for his father with the revelation as to what inspired Robert to enter the legal profession in the first place:

'...If I may be frank, I must confess that, as a rule, one does not look upon an invitation to attend a meeting and make a speech as one of the most welcome of morning visitors. One's natural instinct is to angle in the deep waters of one's engagement book for some plausible excuse, something that will justify a polite expression of regret for being unable to accept it. If one cannot find a decent pretext for declining, and writes accepting the invitation 'with pleasure', one makes what a legal cynic once said was a statement that you would only expect to find in an affidavit; but rules have exceptions, and this is one. I am delighted to bid it welcome as it takes its place in what is already a large and growing family. Here among lawyers, with no laymen to criticise or find fault with us, I am at liberty to say what I believe, that ours is the finest profession in England and that the legal profession in England is the finest in the world. If I was asked to say what it is that has made this country so successful in stumbling out of difficulties into prosperity and making people who hate us and fight against us one day attached and faithful friends the next, I should say that it is because the natural instinct of all Englishmen (in which term I need not say I include Welshmen), is to insist that every man shall have justice whether he is rich or poor, powerful or weak...

I have known Chester and I have known North Wales since my early days. I have no Welsh blood in my veins that I know of – I'm afraid that I haven't sprung from a Welsh bard, proud as I should be to think so – but I always looked upon Wales as my holiday home and I loved it as I have just been saying I love my profession. If I shall not be blamed for being too much of an egotist, I should like to tell you that, with no reason except my affection for the country, I learned to talk Welsh when I was a boy. I wanted to talk to the people I met, the farmers, the shepherds and people of that sort and I learnt to conjugate every verb and almost dislocate my spine by spelling and parsing and pronouncing some of the worst of the Welsh nouns. I should like to recommend this to Dr Sandow as a new treatment for patients who suffer from a weak spine; it would kill or cure. If they stood a course of Welsh grammar they could stand almost anything. I have written dozens of letters in Welsh to an old Welsh friend who first taught me how to shoot and to fish...

At all events, politics and law have this in common, that, no matter what outside advantages a man may have in starting, the doors are wide open to everybody in however humble a position he may begin. The man who knows how to follow the rules of the game and to keep the great traditions of the profession in his mind and in his heart is never debarred from getting from the bottom of the ladder to the top. I knew of one such man in my own personal experience. At the time, he was only a young man filling a humble post at an election in the west of England at one of the polling booths. Now a member of the Bar happened to be standing as a candidate. This gentleman wasn't particularly brilliant but he was very wealthy, had been to a public school and one of the Universities. Furthermore, he had important influences and hosts of friends; in fact, it might be said that the road to the Woolsack was well open to him. Many years later, the young man, who had been helping out at the polling booths, declared to me that this was the moment when it had occurred to him that if the candidate described could get on at the Bar, then why shouldn't he. The difficulty was to find the means to start. He could not afford the fees and his family could certainly not afford to send him there so he went to a solicitor's office, occupied a humble post there for some little time, learnt as much law as he could and ultimately scraped enough together to enable him to join one of the Inns of Court. He had not much left when he had done that but, I believe, by giving lessons to pupils and working hard, he managed to get called to the

Bar. He had also occupied his time by writing a law book, which was a success, and he made a good start. Strangely enough, he told me afterwards that one of the early briefs he held in Court was for the candidate whom he had helped at the polling booths. This gentleman, whose name I would not mention if I knew it, which I don't, found it a difficult case to argue, and, being nervous and diffident, asked his friend to argue it for him. He was a great success, literally and entirely through his own merits. The man I refer to was my own father...

These are the days of union and combination. One man standing alone is at a great disadvantage. It is by mutual help and co-operation that you can tackle difficulties; and it is by associating with your colleagues and getting the advantage of other people's experiences that you can lay up the necessary stores for your own use. I know this Society has a great future before it. I am proud to think that I have been present at this, its first meeting, not exactly to pronounce a forensic benediction over it, but to say a word of friendly and cordial greeting to those who belong to it. If the best of good wishes can secure its success, it will succeed beyond all your expectations. And I hope that when I next come to Chester, your members will have so increased that you will have as much difficulty in accommodating them as the authorities in London have in providing courts for the judges to sit in. In fact, I hope that your members will be so numerous that your large hall itself will not be able to contain them.'

Apart from family holidays to north Wales as a child, Montie continued to visit the country while he was at the Bar. He fished and rented ground for shooting and, undoubtedly, enjoyed the opportunity for practising his Welsh. As he once confessed, his knowledge of the language enabled him to 'keep an eye on the interpreter' when he travelled the Welsh Circuit. And, during the Long Vacation of 1911, it would appear that his sons were involved in a successful rescue attempt at Trearddur Bay which must have delighted him as well as those who were plucked from the heaving waters:

A Timely Rescue

'Among the visitors staying at Trearddur Bay, near Holyhead, are Mr Justice Lush and his family. The judge's two sons were concerned in the timely rescue, a few nights ago, of three visitors who had rowed out into the bay and whose boat capsized. Mr Arthur Lush and Mr Harold Lush with two friends, Messrs Hill and Stewart Browne, who were in two boats, noticed the capsized boat some distance away with its three occupants struggling in the water. Rowing rapidly to the spot, they succeeded, in spite of the very rough sea, in getting the three into their boats. One of the rescued men was in an unconscious state but he soon revived.'

However, only a few weeks after the address at Chester, a water rescue back at Stanmore, where Montie's family now lived, was not so successful. During a party at *Grimsdyke*, at which Montie and Maggie were present, Sir William Gilbert, the famous librettist from the Gilbert and Sullivan partnership, waded into a pond to rescue one of his guests. She happened to be an American actress, aptly named, Ruby Priest, and had, somehow, become entangled in the weeds. Certainly, Gilbert managed to save his guest but, shortly afterwards, suffered a heart attack as a result and died. What a commotion that must have been! And, even today, the *W.S.Gilbert Society* still forms a procession from *Grimsdyke* to *St John's Church*, Stanmore, where he was buried, to mark the exact time of his death.

Having only bought *Tanglewood* in 1910, just a year before this tragedy, I was uncertain as to how well acquainted Montie was with Gilbert. I knew that Montie's eldest daughter, Helen, took singing lessons from Gilbert's adopted daughter and that Montie's youngest daughter, Violet, had happy recollections of playing tennis at *Grimsdyke* before playing at Wimbledon, one of whose founders was her maternal grandfather, Sir Charles Brodie Locock. But exactly when Helen had these lessons is not clear and Violet had not yet been born which would suggest that a more intimate friendship with Gilbert's family only developed after his death. However, I recently discovered from the verger at *St John's* that Montie's family were living at a large house in *Gordon Avenue*, which overlooked the golf course at Stanmore, before they moved to *Tanglewood*. In fact, such was Montie's enthusiasm for golf – he was an avid member of the *Gray's Inn Golfing Society* and was awarded the Captain's Prize in 1908 – that Maggie had insisted on having a huge bell erected on the roof of that house so she could summon him from the course when it was time for lunch. (Apparently, the bell is still *in situ* and may possibly fulfil the same function today!) And, furthermore, Gilbert was frequently involved in litigation battles so it is quite possible that he and Montie had known each other well before the latter moved to *Tanglewood*.

Tanglewood itself was a fourteen-bedroomed house, once occupied by the Countess of Teck, with an expansive garden containing its own tennis court and croquet lawn. It was purchased by Montie for what now seems a ludicrous sum of £2,000 and sold, shortly after his death in 1930, for £10,000 although the Lodge, where Helen, Maurice and Arthur later resided for many years, having first been converted from a stable to a garage and then to a home, was retained by the family until the 1970's. Standing in such beautiful grounds, it must have been a perfect setting for raising a young family and photographs of tennis parties and family groups posing before the test matches at Lords would certainly seem to support that fact. By 1911, Helen would have been sixteen and presumably helpful to her mother when she wasn't developing her musical and artistic talents; Arthur and Harold would have been at *Orley Farm School* with Maurice starting there in a year's time; Bobby would have been beginning to explore the great parameters of the house on his three-year-old legs; and Violet was born in the spring of that year. Where Maggie escaped to when she needed a break from domesticity is not clear but Montie's retreat was, not surprisingly, known as the 'Judgement Room.'

Nevertheless, despite this idyllic family background and a wide range of holiday locations from Anglesey to Southwold and Aviemore to Dulverton on the Somerset/Devon border where his sister, Florence, took salmon fishing on the Exe, Montie was continuing to push himself hard on the Bench. It is known that, shortly after his elevation, he took ill and his involvement in the famous *Cat and Mouse* suffragette trials in 1913-1914 can't have done much to restore his health. Four days after the bombing of

Lloyd-George's new residence at Walton-on-the-Hill in February, 1913, Emmeline Pankhurst, one of the leaders of the suffragettes, was arrested on a charge of having 'counselled and procured' the perpetrators of the crime. She was initially committed for trial at the May Assizes in Guildford but the date and venue was subsequently changed to the 2nd April at the *Central Criminal Court* in London. Not surprisingly, the court was crowded with women and, due to the latest wave of what Mrs Pankhurst's biographer aptly describes as 'guerilla warfare', a large number of policemen were on duty. Messrs Bodkin and Travers Humphreys acted as counsel for the prosecution on behalf of the Crown, Mrs Pankhurst conducted her own defence and Montie was presiding. After he had read the indictment, the defendant pleaded 'not guilty' to wickedly and maliciously inciting women to crime. She then thanked him for courteously inviting her to sit down and for the table which she requested to accommodate her papers.

Mr Bodkin opened the case with an explanation of the 1861 *Malicious Damages to Property Act* and accused Mrs Pankhurst of being an accessory before the fact in relation to the bombing of Lloyd-George's house. He then read out a private letter, written to a friend in her own hand, defending militancy and summarised it as follows: 'If we don't get what we want, the Government and their members will be responsible, and the Government and the public will be bullied into giving us what we want.' Several witnesses were examined and Montie queried the presentation of the case on the grounds that the jury needed to know whether the defendant was being specifically accused of counselling the action of the crime or whether it was the content of her speeches that was acting as a general incitement to damage property. Mr Bodkin replied that the latter assumption was correct and the proceedings continued.

At the close of the examination the following day, Montie asked Mrs Pankhurst if she wanted to call any witnesses herself. She replied that she didn't but wanted to address him instead and, in so doing, raised various objections to what Mr Bodkin had said about her personal circumstances: she didn't ride about in her own motor car while inciting others to commit crimes and suffer the consequences – in fact, she had never owned a car – nor was she earning an income of £1,500 a year from the suffrage movement. She then turned to her own defence and talked at great length about the inadequacy of the country's laws which, by now, many people regarded as being so unjust to women. And, just as she was about to cite some of the misdemeanours of those responsible for upholding the law, Montie had to remind her to stick to the sole question before the jury, i.e. whether or not she was guilty as charged. The final part of her speech primarily concerned itself with why the women were so determined to continue their fight without neglecting to confirm that she would continue her hunger strike if returned to Holloway prison. And she asked the jury to find her not guilty of malicious incitement to a breach of the law. Montie then reiterated the charge and did his summing up:

'It is scarcely necessary for me to tell you that the topics urged by the defendant in her address to you with regard to provocation by the laws of the country and the injustice done to women because they are not given the vote as men are, have no bearing upon the question you have to decide. The motive at the back of her mind, or at the back of the minds of those who actually did put the gunpowder there, would afford no defence to this indictment. I am quite sure you will deal with this case upon the evidence, and the evidence alone, without regard to any question as to whether you think the law is just or unjust. It has nothing to do with the case. I should think you will probably have no doubt that this defendant, if she did these things charged against her, is not actuated by the ordinary selfish motive that leads most of the criminals who are in the dock to commit the crimes that they do commit. She is nonetheless guilty if she did these things which are charged against her although she believes that, by means of this kind, the condition of society will be altered.'

The jury retired to consider their verdict and, once the court was again in session, the foreman delivered a verdict of guilty with a strong recommendation to mercy. And after a final impassioned speech about how the movement would continue until an end was put to what she described as an 'intolerable situation', Montie passed sentence:

'...I can not help pointing out to you that the crime of which you have been convicted is not only a very serious one but, in spite of your motives, is, in fact, a wicked one. It is wicked because it not only leads to the destruction of property of persons who have done you no wrong but, in spite of your calculations, it may expose other people to the danger of being maimed or even killed...I can only say that, although the sentence I am going to pass must be a severe one, it must be adequate to the crime of which you have been found guilty. If you would only realise the wrong you are doing and the mistake you are making and would undertake to amend matters by using your influence in a right direction, I would be the first to use all my best endeavours to bring about a mitigation of the sentence I am about to pass....I have paid regard to the recommendation of the jury. You yourself have stated the maximum sentence (of fourteen years imprisonment) which this particular offence is by the legislature thought to deserve. The least sentence I can pass upon you is a sentence of three years' penal servitude.'

As soon as the sentence was pronounced, pandemonium broke out among the spectators. The murmurs of 'Shame!' quickly swelled into indignant cries from a chorus of women in the gallery and court and some of the women were even screaming while standing on their seats. One woman cried, 'Keep the flag flying!' and others responded with, 'We will! Bravo! Three cheers for Mrs Pankhurst!' The women then filed out of the court singing the *Women's Marseillaise*,

March on, march on,
Face to the dawn,
The dawn of liberty.

while Montie ineffectively threatened them with prison if any woman dared to repeat such a scene. Mrs Pankhurst left the court by a side door and was taken to *Holloway* prison to begin her last sentence. 'In the midst of all this intense excitement,' she says, 'I passed through the grim gates into the twilight of prison, now become a battleground.'

Various members of Asquith's cabinet would have doubtless preferred to have seen Montie pass the maximum sentence, even if that was to be waived at the outbreak of the war when, ironically, a truce by the militants was declared, but two final points may be worthy of consideration: that the tone of Mrs Pankhurst's autobiography bears little hostility towards the judge himself – even the court had remained perfectly calm until the passing of sentence – and that *Tanglewood* escaped totally unscathed. During the early months of that year, golf courses had been sabotaged, telephone cables severed, thousands of windows smashed, the orchid houses at Kew destroyed, the jewel room at the *Tower of London* invaded and the refreshment house at Regent's Park burned to the ground. And, only two months after the trial, such was the spirit of the movement that Emily Davison even threw herself in the path of the galloping horses at Epsom racecourse. She was knocked unconscious and died four days later. Stanmore was certainly not beyond the reach of the militants and one police constable would not have been able to offer much resistance against an angry army of women whose leader Montie had just sent to prison. I may be quite wrong but would like to suggest that Montie's reputation for helping poor women in cases such as the *Furniture Case* and his family connection with the *Mission Hall* and *Regent's Park Chapel* may have played a part in keeping *Tanglewood* secure. Meanwhile, police constable Probert had plenty of time to focus his attention on the pretty, young nanny!

At the outbreak of the First World War, Arthur and Harold were students at *Westminster School* while Maurice, the third eldest son, was at *Harrow* with Maggie's nephew, Charles Bardolf Locock. However, the studies of the two eldest sons were disrupted by the war in 1916: Arthur joined the Motor Transport division of the *British Red Cross Society* and Harold signed up with the Coldstream Guards, briefly serving in occupied Germany and France two years later as a 2nd Lieutenant. Luckily, they returned home safely and were able to continue their education at *Christchurch*, Oxford, where they both matriculated in 1919. What's more, Arthur somehow managed to commandeer an ambulance which the family found very useful for transporting three maids and all their luggage down to Bude for their summer holidays! But Montie's brother, Herbert, was not so lucky. He had already lost his wife, Rose, back in 1890, the same year that Maggie's father and grandfather Pitman died, and, on the 22nd July, 1916, he also lost his only son, Geoffrey, during a

German counter-offensive near Amiens. Geoffrey had reached the rank of Major in the Royal Horse Artillery, had served at Gallipoli with the 29th Division and had been awarded the distinction of *Chevalier of the Legion of Honour*. He was buried at the cemetery at Mailly Wood, nine kilometres north of Albert, with over seven hundred other war casualties.

Florence's younger son, Leslie, also lost his life in France in 1918 but, considering the massive number of fatalities amongst young men during this war, the Lush family was let off fairly lightly, even taking into account the other descendants of the Wiltshire/Dorset community; the only other one I am aware of is Private Herbert Lush of the *Dorset Regiment* who was killed in action on the 9th September, 1914, during another counter-attack following the withdrawal from Mons. He was buried at the British cemetery at Montreuil. Nevertheless, there was one other death only days after the end of the war which must have had a great impact not only on Montie's family and his only surviving brother and sisters but also on the church at Regent's Park. On the 28th November, 1918, Dr Percy Lush breathed his last, not as a result of any wound inflicted on the Western Front but as a consequence of the Great Flu Epidemic which claimed as many as fifty million lives. As I have already mentioned, Percy was one of the pioneers of the *Medical Mission Auxiliary* but he was also actively involved in the work at *Regent's Park Chapel*. He was well-loved and his death somewhat dampened the church community's joy experienced at the signing of the Armistice.

As for the church itself, it had already suffered a major loss in 1883 when Dr Landels, its first pastor for twenty-eight years, resigned and moved to Edinburgh to take up a new post in *Dublin Street*. It was said that not only the death of his son in Genoa in 1879 but also the loss of his closest friends, Robert and Elizabeth, influenced his decision and one can only imagine the effect his resignation must have had on the church. Nevertheless, under the direction of successive pastors, the Reverands Davies, Meyer, Gange and Walker, the work at the Chapel and *Mission Hall* continued to thrive with clubs and classes of all descriptions in which the Lush family played a leading part. Percy was renowned for his teaching in the

Schools and Bible Classes and held the posts of Sunday School Superintendent, Church Elder and Secretary for many years; Montie continued to lead the *Men's Bible Class* as well as widening his net to encompass the *Children's Convalescent Home* at Bushey Heath, the *London Orphan School* at Watford and the *Wealdstone Company of the Church Lads' Brigade*; and the Pearce Goulds were involved in a multitude of activities ranging from Treasurers to Elders and from Chairmen of Public Meetings to Stall Holders at the Annual Sales which were instrumental in supporting the *Home Mission Fund*. Furthermore, the church was closely identified with the building of two new chapels abroad, the *Regent's Park Hall* in Dacca and the *Regent's Park Chapel* in north-west Canada so the church community must have been very busy. However, the Liberal victory of 1906 – the year when the *Regent's Park Chapel* celebrated its Jubilee – represented the peak of the social and political influence of Nonconformity after which the Nonconformist churches shared in the institutional decline of most British churches. And the war that followed certainly took its toll on the Chapel when it 'denuded the church of all its young men while the darkened streets and threat of air raids diminished the congregation.' Had a modification of the terms of the lease, which was about to expire in July, 1922, been successful, the Chapel might have taken on a new lease of life but, sadly, that was not to be. The ground rent of £65 per annum was raised to the astonishing amount of £950 with an additional premium of £596 and the new lease could only be offered for a period of twenty-one years. Therefore, the Elders reluctantly decided that the terms were not acceptable and a public meeting on the 8th May, 1922, after a final Sunday service the day before led by the Rev Frederic Spurr, brought the magnificent work carried out under this roof to a close. And what a terribly sad occasion that must have been even though the *Mission Hall* was still going strong and the *Heath Street Baptist Church* had graciously offered to take it under its wing.

We now move forward to the year 1924 which probably witnessed the most significant case in Montie's career, that of *Harnett v Bond*. It was the first major case of its kind to be associated with the Lunacy Laws and, not surprisingly, attracted a great deal of publicity. The first trial was presided over by Montie and the following summary of the case is taken from the *Lords' Journals*:

'The plaintiff, Mr Harnett, having been received into, and detained as a lunatic in, a house licensed for the reception of lunatics under a duly certified reception order, was granted leave of absence on trial for twenty-eight days. The order granting the leave empowered the manager of the licensed house to take back the plaintiff at any time before the expiration of the said period if his mental condition required it. On the second day of his leave, the plaintiff went to the office of the *Commissioners in Lunacy* and asked to see one of the Commissioners. The Commissioner, after seeing him, telephoned to the manager of the licensed house that the plaintiff was not in a fit state to be at large and detained the plaintiff for two or three hours while the manager sent a motor with two attendants to take him back to the licensed house. Thereafter, the plaintiff was detained in that house and other institutions for lunatics from December 14, 1912, till he escaped on October 15, 1921. He then brought an action against the Commissioner and the manager, charging them jointly and severally with false imprisonment.

The case was tried before a judge and jury. The jury found that the plaintiff, on the day he was taken back, was not of unsound mind or dangerous to himself or others and was fit to be at large; that the Commissioner alone caused him to be detained until the attendants came and did so for the purpose of the plaintiff being detained at the licensed house; and that the manager honestly believed that the plaintiff was of unsound mind and that it was in the plaintiff's interest that he should be taken back to confinement but that he had not exercised reasonable care.

The judge, Mr Justice Lush, directed the jury that it was open to them, if they thought fit, to treat the subsequent long detention of the plaintiff as a direct consequence of the defendants' acts and, as the result of the findings of the jury, gave judgement against the Commissioner for £5000 and against both defendants for £20,000...'

Today, such damages would be considered negligible but, in 1924, they were quite considerable so it was hardly surprising to find that the matter went before the *Court of Appeal* where Montie's judgement was overturned by Lord Justices Scrutton and Bankes on the grounds that the subsequent detention of the plaintiff at the various institutions was not the direct consequence of the Commissioner's action; that there was no foundation for the charge against the manager of detaining the plaintiff without lawful authority; and that there was no evidence to support the finding of the jury that the manager had failed to exercise reasonable care. And their judgement was subsequently affirmed by the *House of Lords*. All the same, there was such a public outrage at the reversal of Montie's judgement that a Royal Commission was demanded, and granted. The following sample of letters, many of which evoke a great deal of sympathy for their writers as well as Mr Harnett, give a strong indication of the public mood at the time. You may also observe that those letters written by patients show precious little in the way of incoherence which might be attributed to people really suffering from mental illness:

Ladies' Imperial Club,
9, Arlington Street,
Piccadilly,
S.W.1.
February 29, 1924

Dear Sir,

May I express to you my admiration of the humane, <u>Christian</u> manner in which you have conducted the Harnett case?

In your court listening were perhaps a dozen people who have themselves suffered under the Lunacy Laws or who have relatives <u>now</u> oppressed and terrified by them. The gross iniquity of what is going on in our beloved England because of the ignorance, indifference, callousness and <u>inhumanity</u> of those who administer these laws will be revealed when the urgently needed Royal Commission is appointed. May <u>you</u> be the judge to preside over it!

If you have not read 'The Experiences of an Asylum Patient' with an Introduction by Dr Montagu Lomax (published by Allen and Unwin, who also publish his 'Experiences of an Asylum Doctor'), I wish that you could read it. The writer – a lady whom I have met – was for <u>twelve</u> years incarcerated in five asylums and (sane all the time) subjected to treatment which is almost unprintable.

Yours sincerely,

C.W.

38, Kimberley Rd,
Bournemouth.
May 17, 1924

<u>Mr Justice Lush.</u>

Sir,

Is there anything that an ordinary member of the public can do to shake the confidence of the community in the present day mental experts? You must admit yourself that, despite the facts brought forward, the nation does not want to believe that we have in charge of our mental hospitals a set of experts who do not know their job.

I was in a mental hospital for eleven months and only got out by the skin of my teeth. This was four years ago but I have never forgotten my experience. I made three books of notes while there and have been able to supply Dr Montagu Lomax with instances of ill-treatment. But the point is that the whole system is wrong; the patients are made worse instead of better and the experts haven't the honesty to admit the failure of their treatment.

Mr Justice Lush, you deserve to be blessed by every poor person shut behind asylum bars for your outspoken words when trying the Harnett case. You will live to see your verdict justified and a complete reform of the treatment of so-called insane persons.

Yours faithfully,

D.M.

Villa 6,
L.C.C. Mental Hospital,
New Southgate.
May 22, 1924

To:-
His Worship, Justice Lush.

Your Worship,

We sane people here followed with great interest the wonderful way with which you handled the 'Harnett' case. To us it was a joy to find there was one just judge left in England.

No amount of compensation can make up to any man or woman for the mental suffering they are compelled to endure in lunatic asylums. 'Luna' is the Latin word for 'moon'. 'Lunacy' therefore means 'moonstruck.' Even if the name 'Colney Hatch' has been changed into 'Mental Hospital' it is a mental hospital governed by the Lunacy Act. That act has not been changed.

I myself, just a year ago today, was told I was on the edge of a nervous break-down. Without being told where I was going, I was brought here from St Pancras in an ambulance. When put to bed I enquired where I was. The answer was New Southgate. That answer conveyed nothing to me because I do not know the locality. When, after eight days or so, I was allowed to get up, I saw the words Colney Hatch printed up in the Cloak Room. For a few seconds I was petrified with horror and after that it was no longer the edge. I was over the edge. I conjured up all that I had heard about mad people and what I went through mentally is known to my Creator and myself alone.

And, as I am alone in the world, I suppose I shall have to spend the rest of my life here. The thing seems incredible especially here in England. All kinds of conditions are thrown together – from gentlewomen suffering with nerves to women from Holloway jail. Language of the most offensive and indelicate kind is here our daily portion and, if we can't sleep at night, our nightly portion.

Whatever Justice Bankes may say, we, who have been through the mill, know that your verdict in the 'Harnett Case' was just, and we can at least hope that something will be done to differentiate between shattered nerves and lunacy.

Yours most Respectfully,

U. B.

Scalebor Park Mental Hospital,
Burley in Wharfedale,
Leeds.
May 16, 1925

Dear Sir,

Although the Lords have settled the appeal in the way they have, there is to my mind gratitude due to yourself for plain words which helped very materially to bring about the present Commission of Enquiry. You may have 'lost the day' in a present-time sense but you have won the morale of the trial by bringing to use rightful arguments. I, for one, thank you, Sir.

For Mr Harnett I am very sympathetic that he should be such a great loser financially. He deserves, I consider, a public subscription fund raising.

Yours respectfully,

J. W.

The letter from Mr Harnett himself is distinctly marked 'private' so it would not do to reproduce it here but you will not be surprised to hear how appreciative he was of Montie's moral support. However, I will reproduce the words of Montie's bard:

'LINES

written on an English jury punishing an infraction of the liberty of the subject by a verdict of £25,000 damages. (Inscribed to one of the greatest of the English judicial names.)

Not idly as the symbol of our Law
A Lion rampant guards an ancient crown;
Once more that tireless warden hath struck down
New gaolers on the old with puissant paw.
This is thy glory, England; this, the awe
Which thrills all lesser lands that mark the seed
Of those, who on the eyot of Runnymede,
Drew up thy deathless Charta without flaw.
Thou loveliest child of Freedom! Greece nor Rome
Nor later races styled republican
In happiest hour set sentries such as thine –
Not even thy daughter of the Western foam –
Nor viewed a tyrant veil the Rights of Man
With the swift anger of thine eyes divine!

LEX.'

In the letter to Montie's eldest son, from which I have already quoted, the poet mentions sending some prints of this 'poor sonnet' to Montie which were gratefully acknowledged by the recipient. Indeed, both Montie and Percy were no mean poets themselves but, since the bulk of their output was written in Greek or Latin, I shall make do with the opening lines of one of the former's poems written for his *Classical Tripos* at Cambridge and offer you a 'poor' translation. Even those not familiar with the Latin language might recognise that 'peculiarly melodious quality' of his voice which, in fact, is quite lost in the translation:

Suaviter o libans nitidos aestatis odores,
Libera per dulces expatiabar agros.

Sweetly tasting the blooming scents of summer,
I freely roamed through the charming fields.

I have already alluded to the state of Montie's health as far back as 1906 but, in 1922, after a series of interruptions to his career on the Bench, he underwent a serious operation and there can be little doubt that his personal attachment to such a sensitive case as *Harnett v Bond* did little to aid his recovery. By now he was seventy-two and, undoubtedly prompted by Maggie, he decided to call it a day on the Bench. In May, 1925, he handed in his resignation and, a month later, was appointed a Member of the *Privy Council*. In fact, his health was such that even that appointment had to be delayed but, even though he hadn't equalled his father's status in the *Court of Appeal*, this was an honour which they both shared and was undoubtedly one that he felt privileged to accept. The following passages pay tribute to his illustrious career:

The Daily Chronicle:

'There are men who typify the best traditions of the profession they adorn. When they pass from positions of public importance, their achievement calls for appraisement. When their withdrawal synchronises with the passing away of great traditions of service, it is the more necessary to note the event. The retirement of Mr Justice Lush deserves comment from the personal and public standpoints.

Although his resignation from the King's Bench Division is due to continuing physical weakness, it is hoped that he will be able to serve on the Judicial Committee of the Privy Council. His ripe judgement and deep learning in the law, with his unfailing and even gentle courtesy, will be welcome in Downing Street.

Sir Montague Lush was brought up in the spartan methods of the Victorian Bar. He plodded through dull papers with meticulous care. He attended to the Law Reports with exemplary diligence. He addressed his Majesty's judges with studied courtesy and treated his clients as persons deserving respect. His attitude towards fellow-practitioners, even of the lowest standing, was that of a perfect English gentleman.

He came of a remarkable legal stock and his father, as a Lord Justice, was a model he strove unceasingly to emulate. Sir Montague became a public servant of considerable parts and he applied himself to duty with unremitting toil. It is no secret that he was deeply impressed by the evidence of conditions in mental establishments during a recent notorious trial and his sensitive spirit was acutely affected by some of the revelations. After delivering judgement in that case, he spoke with concern about its effect upon his mind...To have filled a seat on the bench in the High Court of Justice is a distinction that is not always enhanced but Lush J. withdraws from judicial office with the affection of his fellow-lawyers and the respect of the discerning public.'

Dundee Courier:

'Owing to what may be called super-conscientiousness, Mr Justice Lush, who has retired, was a judge whose cases rarely came to an abrupt conclusion. He was determined to let the side with the worse case have its full say. He thus did not maintain on the Bench the reputation for dash that he won as a Silk. When he was at the Bar there was no more dreaded cross-examiner. He went for hostile witnesses like a bull terrier, and his fighting capacity was combined with a profound knowledge of the law.'

The Law Journal:

'...Particularly we shall miss Mr Justice Lush than whom no kinder and more courteous man ever presided over His Majesty's Assize. There is no other word for it; he was always charming. Of his high efficiency there was never any doubt: his method and his manner were, to say the least, unique. He carried from the Bar his amazing gift of putting a deadly question to a lying witness in a most gentle and least aggressive form. To the shy but truthful witness he afforded the invariable encouragement of an almost affectionate sympathy. We at the Bar hardly ever saw him angry: under the extreme provocation of a too persistent fallacy, the most that would happen would be that a note of slight irritation would creep into his discourse. Though all of us must approve, and congratulate him upon the honour now conferred on him, we must all regret that witness actions are not tried by the Judicial Committee of the Privy Council.'

Evening Standard:

'Sir Charles Lush, who is now to retire after fifteen years on the Bench, is a remarkable example of legal heredity. His father, Sir Robert Lush, was one of the first Lord Justices of Appeal and, only last year, two of his sons were called at Gray's Inn on the same night. Like all good judges, he knows how, on occasion, to exploit the valuable quality of judicial ignorance. I remember a case some years ago in which, having first inquired what a 'jumper' was, he then asked what might be the meaning of the word 'lingerie' and displayed much earnestness in seeking information about these two remarkable expressions.'

Nottingham Post:

'...Of late years, deafness has been his greatest handicap though, sometimes, I have suspected, when watching him try cases, that he has made cunning use of his disability by slightly exaggerating it. Often he would politely ask a witness to repeat the answer to some question and then apologetically to repeat it again. And, sometimes, there would be a variation in the answers which a prompt detection by the judge betrayed that he had not been quite so deaf after all! Another very effective little trick of his in checking careless answers by witnesses who appeared to be replying 'Yes' or 'No' to counsel's questions automatically would be suddenly to interject: 'What was that question you said 'Yes' to?"

If Montie's industry had taken its toll on his health, the question might be raised as to the effect it had on Maggie's. Surely she must have tried to persuade him to slow down and indulge himself a little more with his leisure pursuits but, finding that this was a lost cause, suffered more than just a little frustration herself. Indeed, during his highly active life, she must have been just as active herself. Not only did she have a large household to run with a substantial family to raise but looking after such a spirited and industrious husband must have been quite a tall order for any gentle, Christian wife. Sadly, towards the end of November, 1925, she was taken ill with flu and, on the 4th December, passed away at the age of only fifty-three.

The impact of Montie's bereavement can only have equalled the loss felt by his own father when Elizabeth died. They had both depended heavily on the inner strength, moral support and spiritual love of their wives so it will come as no surprise to hear that Montie's own health remained in a precarious state for the next five years. Of course, all the family rallied round him and he was well looked after by two male nurses, Lothian and McKay, but his sensitive soul had been shattered beyond repair. At the time of Maggie's death, his flame of life was already beginning to flicker and, on Sunday the 22nd June, 1930, it flickered no more. The saga of *Like Father Like Son* had finally come to an end.

The following Wednesday, Montie's funeral took place at *St John's Church*, Stanmore, conducted by the Revs Hewett and Bernays. As the cortege left the church, the *Nunc Dimittis* was chanted by the choir and the organist, R.E.H.Springett, played Chopin's *Funeral March*. The interment was in the grave of his beloved wife and the grave was lined with roses, carnations, ferns and yew branches. And, needless to say, in addition to a large family attendance there were representatives from all the societies he had patronised as well as many of his judicial friends and colleagues, including Lady Gilbert and Mr Davies who had been his clerk for thirty years.

Most of Montie's tributes were recorded on his retirement and, from these, I have already quoted a fair sample. So, without running the risk of repeating myself, I will close my appraisal of his remarkable life with these headlines from the *Evening News,*

DEATH OF THE JUDGE WHO NEVER LOST HIS TEMPER

TACT AND TENACITY OF SIR MONTAGUE LUSH

LITTLE MAN WITH BIG REPUTATION

WHAT IS A JUMPER?

AUTHOR OF 'THE LAW OF HUSBAND AND WIFE'

the final paragraph of the bard's letter to Arthur:

'To the end, his beautiful voice and impassioned eloquence will ring in my ears; to the end, the noble vision of his presence, both as advocate and judge, will subsist. And I believe that not since Romilly sank into his tomb has a kindlier or more generous heart sanctified, and with mercy sweetened, the Bench of England.'

and the title afforded him by *Vanity Fair* other than the title of this book:

'Worthy Son of a Worthy Sire.'

The Rt Hon Sir Charles Montague Lush, PC
in
'Like Father like Son'

Vanity Fair's Men of the Day, 18th January, 1911

Postlude

Florence also died in 1930 but, as I have already mentioned, her descendants continued to take a keen interest in all the work at the *Mission Hall* until it closed in the 1970's and at *Heath Street Baptist* Church until the present day. Herbert, Montie's only surviving brother at the time of his death, was knighted in 1923 and ended his days at the age of ninety-one in a nursing home at Stanmore. And as for Montie's children, interestingly, only the two daughters ever married, Helen to Eric Neville-Heaney in 1937 (he died only four years later), and Violet to Basil Sheldon in 1935 and to Robert Kirkpatrick Nuttall in 1974. (As a matter of interest, Robert's first wife, Evelyn Hopwood, was the great granddaughter of the literary critic, George Henry Lewes, who spent much of his life with George Eliot, and Robert himself is a distant cousin of Empress Eugenie whose only son, the Prince Imperial, Sir Charles Locock delivered in the previous century. Robert promises me a position at the French Court after the next Revolution!) As for Montie's unmarried sons, Arthur was another conscientious barrister who reached the age of eighty-nine; he was a keen aviator and, during the 1930's, kept his own bi-plane at Hatfield. Harold, a keen motorcyclist, diversified from his legal background and worked for *Lloyds* until his life was tragically cut short by septicaemia in 1934. Maurice also diversified on account of his asthma attacks and spent much of his time writing for the law journals. And Bobby, a talented jazz pianist with 'a mischievous face', became a successful solicitor until his life also ended prematurely following a bungled surgical operation in 1966.

Appendix

Some other notable Lushes:

1. George William Lush (b1881, Poole, d1926, Parkstone), son of a prosperous corn merchant in Parkstone, Dorset, joined the *Queen's Own Dorset Yeomanry*, fought in the Boer War, treated as local hero and granted Freedom of the Borough of Poole in 1901.

2. Venerable John Arthur Lush (b1882, Dorset d1964, Invercargill), Vicar of *St John's Church*, Invercargill, and Archdeacon of Southland.

3. Brigadier Maurice Stanley Lush, CB,CBE, MC, 6th Earl of Limerick (b1896, d2003), *Royal Artillery*, 1915-19, Egyptian Army, 1919-22, Governor of North Province, Sudan, 1938-41, Chief Political Officer in Ethiopea, 1941-42, Military Administrator of Madagascar, 1942, Executive Commissioner and Vice-President of *Allied Commission*, Haly, 1943-46, Resident Representative for Germany and Austria of *Intergovernmental Committee on Refugees*, 1946-47, *Chief of Mission in the Middle East*, 1949-51, Vice-President of the *British and Foreign Bible Society. Commander of the Order of the Knights of Malta*, 1915; CB, 1944; CBE, 1942; *Order of the Nile*; *Officer of the Legion of Merit*, USA, 1945. He was present at Montie's funeral.

4. Sir Archibald James (b1900, Tredgar, d1976, Abergavenny), Chief Inspector of Schools for Monmouthshire and Chairman of *Welsh Hospital Board*. Knighted, 1969.

5. Ernest Henry Lush (b1908, Bournemouth, d1988, Harrogate), piano pupil of Tobias Matthay, BBC staff pianist and accompanist, from 1927, also famous recitalist and concerto soloist who performed in the *Henry Wood Promenade Concerts*.

6. Hon Sir George Herman Lush, Kt, (b1912), *Melbourne University*, called to Victorian Bar, 1935, Lecturer in Mercantile Law at *Melbourne University*, 1947-55, QC Victoria, 1957,

Chairman of the *Victorian Bar Council*, 1964-66, Chancellor of *Monash University*, 1983. Knighted, 1979. Judge of the *Supreme Court of Victoria*.

7. Christopher Duncan Lush, CMG, (b1928), *Magdalen College*, Oxford, called to the Bar at *Gray's Inn*, 1953, Assistant Legal Adviser to the *Foreign Office*, 1959-62, Deputy Political Adviser for Berlin, 1965-66, Head of Chancery in Amman, 1969-71, Counsellor in Paris and Vienna, 1974-82, Permanent Representative to the *Council of Europe*, Strasbourg, since 1983. CMG, 1983.

8. Sylvia Rosalind Pery (née Lush), Countess of Limerick, (b1935), eldest daughter of Maurice Stanley Lush, ed. *St Swithin's*, Winchester and *Lady Margaret Hall*, Oxford, married Viscount Glentworth in 1961.

Printed in Great Britain
by Amazon